## Praise for Joanna Brooks and *The Book of Mormon Girl*

"This is an utterly necessary memoir."

—Carolyn Forché, celebrated poet and human rights activist

"Joanna Brooks sheds the candid, genuinely informative light I've been looking for on this 'Mormon moment' in American life."

—Krista Tippett, host of American Public Media's *On Being*

"This story is beautifully, universally true. It gives me hope. Hope for our miscounted daughters, for our misunderstood grandmothers, and for the achingly faithful hearts, like mine, still beating and bleeding for peace, tolerance, and the seemingly lost cause of human respect. It gives me hope for our common lineage: love."

—Karen Maezen Miller, author of *Momma Zen: Walking the Crooked Path of Motherhood* and *Hand Wash Cold: Care Instructions for an Ordinary Life*

"Joanna Brooks captures Mormonism in revealing but tender ways that are sure to resonate with insiders and outsiders alike. Mormonism may not yet have found its Chaim Potok, but it has its Joanna Brooks."

—R. B. Scott, author of *Mitt Romney: An Inside Look at the Man and His Politics*

"Joanna Brooks defies Mormon stereotypes."

—Politico.com

"Laugh-out-loud funny and break-your-heart poignant, *The Book of Mormon Girl* delivers an ironic triumph: a little girl's religion invests her with enough history, bravery, and devotion that the woman she becomes can only stand up to her people and say, 'No! We are better than that!' A delicious and hopeful journey."

—Carol Lynn Pearson, author of *Mother Wove the Morning* and *No More Goodbyes: Circling the Wagons Around Our Gay Loved Ones*

"Joanna Brooks draws upon a rich spiritual legacy in this compelling memoir of being found and lost and found again. What she describes as a 'fierce and hungry faith' leaps off the page with passion, galvanizing readers who strive for justice and want to live their religion on their own terms. She is a contemporary Mormon pioneer."

—Jana Riess, author of *Flunking Sainthood* and *Mormonism for Dummies*

"Joanna Brooks's narrative is, by turns, disarming, funny, wrenching, and inspiring. Steeped in the quaint, nourishing ways of a Southern California Mormon home, she was a 'root beer among the Cokes' of her non-Mormon schoolmates: sparkling, different, no caffeine. She grew up and grew conflicted, finding herself in a decade-long exile from her conservative people. Badly wanting her daughters to know what her grandmothers knew, to lay claim to the curious beauty and power of her religious heritage, Brooks at last declares herself 'not an enemy': 'I will not be disappeared from the faith of my ancestors.' She returns as a Coke among Mormon root beers: still different, still sparkling. Her version of the Mormon story is unorthodox, uncommon, and lyrical. This is a quietly fierce, authentic, and faithful voice, one that insists her religious tradition is young, and the next chapter yet to be written."

—Philip Barlow, Arrington Chair of
Mormon History and Culture,
Utah State University

*f*P

# the book of mormon girl

## a memoir of an american faith

joanna brooks

FREE PRESS
New York London Toronto Sydney New Delhi

Free Press
A Division of Simon & Schuster, Inc.
1230 Avenue of the Americas
New York, NY 10020



This Free Press trade paperback edition August 2012



Manufactured in the United States of America

5 7 9 10 8 6 4

Library of Congress Cataloging-in-Publication Data is available.

ISBN 978-1-4516-9968-5
ISBN 978-1-4516-9969-2 (ebook)

*for ella and rosa*

# contents


| | | |
|---|---|---|
| **1** | plan of salvation | **1** |
| **2** | sparkling difference | **13** |
| **3** | signs of the times | **29** |
| **4** | *marie osmond's guide to beauty, health & style* | **47** |
| **5** | mormons vs. born-agains—dance-off, rose bowl, 1985 | **67** |
| **6** | sister williams's tampons | **83** |
| **7** | object lessons | **99** |
| **8** | files | **113** |
| **9** | sealed portion | **143** |
| **10** | pioneer day | **145** |
| **11** | protect marriage | **161** |
| **12** | gathering the tribes | **181** |
| **13** | the book of mormon girl | **199** |
| | acknowledgments | **205** |
| | reading group guide | **211** |

# the book of mormon girl

# 1

# plan of salvation

On Monday nights, my father and mother gathered their four children around the kitchen table in our tract house on the edge of the orange groves and taught us how the universe worked.

Sometimes they used a stack of cotton work gloves to demonstrate the thin illusoriness of this life. "Your spirit is like this hand," my father would say, wiggling his fingers. "Your spirit has always existed. When you were born, your spirit went into your body and a veil of forgetfulness was drawn across your mind." He slipped his hand into the glove. "When you die your spirit will leave your body and join the spirits of your ancestors on the other side of the veil," he said, withdrawing his hand from the glove, and leaving it an inert heap on the Formica tabletop. Death was made as small and familiar to me as changing clothes, and this life a moment of forgetfulness on a long, long thread of being.

Sometimes too my parents taught us about the farm-boy prophet Joseph Smith, who long ago in upstate New York had gone into a grove of trees, gotten down on his knees, and put his questions directly to God, who, with His son Jesus, appeared directly to Joseph Smith and then sent angels to reveal new books of scripture and new ways of being. Every night when I knelt on the little crocheted orange prayer rug at the side of my bed, I prayed to a God that heard and answered. Sometimes too I had dreams and God spoke kindly to me in my dreams, and I woke with wet eyes, so disappointed to be back on the forgetful side of the veil that separated this world from the next.

When we children were asleep, my auburn-haired mother stayed up late, late, late, pulling the names of our ancestors out of thickets of old records, to reorder them all for eternity's sake in a baby-blue Book of Remembrance with the outlines of Mormon temple spires embossed on the cover in gold. Sometimes, in the morning, standing in the kitchen, she would tell us how dark forces had surrounded her late at night to encumber her work, but our ancestors stepped through time, straight through the walls of our tract house in the orange groves, identifying themselves by name and declaring that they would protect her.

I grew up in kitchens where bushels of backyard-grown green beans were canned and put up for the winter, habits of pioneer preparedness, steam on the kitchen windows against the perfect California sunshine outside. On the refrigerator hung a calendar from the local Mormon mortuary, each month a picture of a different Mormon temple around the globe: in Arizona, London, Switzerland, or Los Angeles. I grew up riding in fleets of blue-paneled family vans, bench seats loaded with children, all going to church in our playclothes on a Wednesday afternoon, everything perfectly understood among us, all the lyrics memorized, nothing to be explained.

Early on Sunday mornings, the fourteen-year-old boys from church knocked on our front door to gather in the tithes and offerings. Later, my parents, brother, sisters, and I sat together in wooden pews, sang pioneer hymns, and took a white-bread-and-tap-water sacrament passed on plastic trays. On Sunday afternoons, my father, who worked all week as an engineer but gave his weekends to service as the bishop of our congregation, stayed behind to hear all the confessions and woes of the people: all their secrets he tucked away in the breast pocket of his polyester Sunday suit. And most Sunday evenings, seventy-something-year-old Sister Pierce would appear on our doorstep, a homemade strawberry pie in her hands, an offering to my father, the bishop, who one midnight in a cold hospital room had anointed her head with consecrated olive oil and given her a healing blessing.

This is how I came into this world, into this world of believing: an ancient spirit striving to remember the shape of eternity at the kitchen table, in a house where ancestors knew our names and stepped through the walls, my dreams filled with light, my head consecrated with oil, every Sunday morning white bread and tap water for sacrament, every Sunday evening the taste of a ripe glazed strawberry saying "grateful" on my tongue.

When I turned seven years old, my father asked me if I could read the whole Book of Mormon before I was to be baptized at age eight. And I said I could. So every night my father settled in beside me in my little twin bed on the second story of the tract home at the edge of the orange groves, and we held the Book of Mormon on our laps.

Together, we read of a small family of Israelites, Lehi and Sariah, their children Laman, Lemuel, Nephi, and Sam, warned by God to leave the land of their ancestors and travel far across the oceans to the Americas, where they would become (as we believed) the ancestors of the American Indians.

We read of a powerful dream given by God to Lehi. Lehi dreamed that he traveled for hours in dark mists of uncertainty, begging for mercy from God, until he reached a beautiful field, with a river and a tree of life bearing delicious fruit. A narrow path with an iron handrail led to the tree of life, past great and spacious buildings of people in fancy clothes who mocked the searching humility of Lehi, his family, and the numberless masses of people who pressed forward along the path, hungry for the delicious fruit. How many strayed from the path and were lost in the mists, or joined the proud crowds in the great and spacious building! How few finally held to the iron handrail and made it to the tree of life!

And as I felt the warmth of my father in bed beside me, I also felt the terrible danger of the world around us, peril rushing in currents beneath us, threatening to separate us one from another, and the threat of that separation was to my mind unbearable. My father understood the terrible danger too, and he hungered for some way to get me safely through the mists crowding in around us. Mormonism was the name of the iron handrail that would lead us through these mists to that beautiful tree, the end of all our hungers.

For I had been born of goodly parents who, in the wilderness of the late twentieth century, saw the wreckage of empires, markets, and civilizations, but did not know how to disentangle effects from causes, nor had the vocabulary to name the strands of these knotted histories, nor their place in them, nor the mundane and disastrous traumas of their own common American upbringings, nor the mundane and disastrous traumas lived by a millennium's worth of their poor and common ancestors, and who heard all around them mocking crowds like faceless laugh tracks of sitcom television threatening oblivion.

Every night in my second-story room in the tract house in Orange County the year before I was baptized, my father and I read the Book of Mormon, the stories of ancient Israelite peoples led by God to the Americas, and their wars, visions, and wanderings. No one else in the world believed in the Book of Mormon but Mormons like us. So we huddled together, my nursing father and me, safe in tender longing, as the currents and the garbage and the television laugh tracks ran down the streets and fell into the storm drains and rushed along the concreted river channels, alongside the freeways, past abandoned orange groves, out to the black and trackless sea.

In those days we Mormons, most of us, were not a wealthy people. We were people one or two generations from the alfalfa farm, or the homestead. We were high school teachers, bookkeepers, nurses, engineers, and mechanics, people who fed eight children on bread homemade from wheat stored in great tins in the garage and milk reconstituted from powder. And in addition to the 10 percent of our incomes we dutifully tithed to build temples around the world, the offerings we paid the first Sunday of every month when we skipped two meals to provide for the poor among us, and the pennies we collected for the Mormon children's hospital in Salt Lake City, we raised money to construct our own church buildings.

I had heard the stories of long ago that when Mormons built their first sacred temple at Kirtland, Ohio, from timber and local sandstone, Mormon women smashed their dishes and glasses to press into the plaster so that it would sparkle in the sun. In the 1970s, when Mormons were building meetinghouses across North America, our grown-ups came up with all sorts of homely schemes to pay into the building fund. Our mothers baked dozens of pumpkin pies for a church Thanksgiving supper and then bought them back one slice at a time for us to eat on paper plates at the ward-house supper. Our fathers volunteered to drive Hertz rental cars from one airport to another, collecting ten dollars an hour to help the agencies sort out their inventories. And every year my father, being bishop, organized a holiday bazaar where we could sell our homemade crafts to one another: gingerbread houses, jars of peach preserves, handmade pioneer bonnets.

Sister Simmons was in her eighties, a widow, Utah-born, one of the numberless Mormons who moved down to California during the Depression, or the War, seeking work. She told my father she wanted to do her part for the building fund.

"What are your talents?" my father asked from his seat behind the desk in the bishop's office.

"I can crochet," Sister Simmons said. "Though it takes me a while."

"Well, that's fine," my father said. "Why don't you make a real nice afghan, Sister Simmons, and we'll make it the centerpiece of the night. We'll put it up for a silent auction."

What materialized at the bazaar was the ugliest afghan

my father had ever seen: alternating chevrons of burnt umber and brassy yellow, with a brassy yellow fringe.

But who would dare say a word to Sister Simmons? So proud of her dedicated labors: her eighty-year-old hands curling around their crochet hooks as she sat in the soft chair in front of the television in her little house on the edge of a concrete river on the alluvial plains of Southern California, her devotion galvanizing into purpose, while her children are all grown, her husband is gone and waiting to call her name and bring her across the veil into heaven, while leggy blondes in short shorts and espadrilles bounce across the screen of the little television, and the laugh track issues forth in random little bursts, faceless and sort of menacing.

So my father put the afghan on display and set out the bid sheet.

Late in the evening he saw that no one had bid. Not one single bid.

He looked at my mother across the room, as she supervised us four children, pushing Jell-O salads across our paper plates with plastic forks. And then he wrote a number down on the bid sheet: *$100.* A lot of money in those days.

But how Sister Simmons smiled when she stopped by the table where her afghan was displayed and spied the $100 figure on her bid sheet. And how proud she felt that by the labors of her hands she had transformed burnt umber and brassy yellow acrylic yarn into a sacred offering, a handsome sum for the building fund.

You will say these are treacly widow's mite stories, and I will say, yes, they are. But this is how I first came to understand what a story is, and how to define salvation: salvation is the eye that sees in secret and rewards the labors of homely hands. Salvation is the steady work of elderly women who remember the long avenues in Utah lined with cottonwood trees, and their fathers working their hands rough on the local ward house, or the Mormon Tabernacle in Salt Lake City. What was there to compare to this feeling of belonging to one another, belonging to the only people who believed as we believed, as our mothers and fathers, and pioneer grandmothers and grandfathers believed, safe from the mocking and fashionable faceless crowds, safe where no one would say your books of scripture are all made up, or the sacred undergarments you promised to wear every day are funny, or your afghan is too ugly, or, old woman, there is nothing in you the world loves anymore.

This is the world I willingly joined when at eight years old I put on a white dress with a Peter Pan collar sewn with special intention and purpose by my Utah-born grandmother and stepped to the edge of a font of turquoise-blue water, where my father, dressed in an all-white suit, stood waist deep in the water and beckoned me to come. He placed one of his arms around my narrow shoulders and prayed, "I baptize you in the name of the Father, and the Son, and the Holy Ghost."

I squeezed my eyes tight as he lowered me entirely into the water, as special witnesses watched from beside the font to make sure that the immersion was total. Not a thread of my white dress or a filament of my dark brown hair floated to the top in this perfect enactment of my own death, my own passage through the veil.

This is the world I joined when I stepped from the font into the towel held by my mother, who, with my grandmother, fussed over my wet hair and helped me change into dry clothes in the church bathroom so that I could once again go out into the embrace of friends and family, take my seat, and have the hands of my father come down upon my head and with his words command the Holy Ghost as my companion, to walk beside me, an invisible guide and guardian. This is the great sweet weight I felt being a member of the Church of Jesus Christ of Latter-day Saints, a Mormon not just by birth but also by choice and baptism, making and keeping sacred promises, a member of a people chosen because we had chosen to be ourselves.

I grew up in a world where all the stories I heard arrived at the same conclusions: the wayfarer restored, the sick healed, the lost keys found, a singular truth confirmed. And an orthodox Mormon story is the only kind of story I ever wanted to be able to tell.

But these are not the kinds of stories life has given me.

Every Mormon carries with them a bundle of stories like a suitcase of family secrets. Polygamous ancestors we have learned to be ashamed of. Histories that reveal the human flaws of the ones who came before us. Doctrines we dare not mention in public for fear of ridicule. Sacrifices we refuse to believe God would ask of us. Stories of loss that do not end neatly with restoration and stories of leaving that do not conclude with the return home.

In the world I grew up in, it was not okay to tell unorthodox stories. We did not hear them in church. We did not read them in scripture. But sooner or later they break through to the surface in every Mormon life, in every human life, in every life of faith. I am not afraid of them. Because this is the story life has given me to tell.

# 2

# sparkling difference

Growing up in Southern California—outside the Utah precincts of our Zion, our lovely Deseret—I was almost always the only Mormon girl in the room. I knew this because everywhere I went, I looked for other Mormons. The first day of third grade, I sat at my desk and counted head by head, red, blond, and brown: how many of my deskmates did I go to church with? Whose parents did I call "Brother" and "Sister" and whose "Mr." and "Mrs."? Which ones knew all the Book of Mormon stories, or spent their summer vacations with Utah cousins, or piled their old clothes into bundles for the Deseret Industries, our special chain of Mormon thrift stores across the American West? In my third-grade classroom, I was the only one.

And when I went to birthday parties, I made sure to check if I was the only Mormon girl. For then I would have to ask if

I could please have a root beer instead of a Coca-Cola like all the other children were having. Because it was our rule that we did not drink Coca-Cola, or Dr Pepper, or Mountain Dew, or Sunkist (the only orange soda with caffeine), or even Aspen soda, the new apple-flavored soda they advertised on television with the pretty blond skier going down the powdery slope to communicate its deep refreshment. That Aspen soda sure looked beyond delicious, but it was not to be.

For these were our rules: No tea. No coffee. No cigarettes. No alcohol of any kind. No caffeine. Which is how I became an expert in the world of American sodas, knowing that those cardboard flats of grocery-store-brand orange, grape, and strawberry sodas, the root beers, ginger ales, and 7UPs were all beloved of God and the Mormons, while all others containing caffeine were strictly off limits. This is how I learned to discipline my appetites around the words of the prophets.

When I went to the large birthday parties at the local ice cream parlor with the faux stained-glass windows, red vinyl booths, and marble tabletops, it was up to me to whisper to one of the parents: "No Coke, please; only root beer, thank you." There was no need to explain such things when I went to the birthdays of Juli, or Shayne, or the other Mormon girls at my school. There was no need to explain at all, no waiting in nervous anticipation for the big tray of sodas to arrive, fifteen identical glasses of bubbly soda and who would stop to help me find out which one—not the waitress, and not the parents busy with so many children. It was up to me alone to figure out how to locate the no-caffeine soda without risking so much as a taste of a Coke, maybe just smell the drinks, or rather go totally without—yes, no problem. The challenge of it all raised a simple birthday party refreshment into something of a sacred offering.

Yes, to tell the truth, I loved being a Mormon girl, a root beer among the Cokes. I relished my sparkling internal difference, all but invisible to the untrained eye.

Invisible as our differences might have been to the non-Mormons we lived among, we Mormons were never invisible to one another, especially in the Book of Mormon belt, the sacred geographical domain that ran south from Canada down through Idaho, Utah, and Nevada to Arizona, then west into Southern California and my home at the edge of the orange groves. Even in airports, gas stations, and department stores, we Mormons could spot other Mormons: married people with several children in tow; always modestly dressed, our dresses and shorts to the knees, our shoulders covered, the shadow of the neckline or hemline of our sacred undergarments barely visible through the clothes; our faces soft and pale from the church commitments that kept us indoors most of the weekend; our men clean-shaven and sort of girlish because they were free of vices, and still wearing haircuts short as missionaries'; never a curse word uttered, never a Coke or a coffee or cigarette in hand. Maybe driving a two-toned blue passenger van with bench seats, and always carrying an extra book of scripture: never just the Bible but our Book of Mormon too.

We could identify other Mormons just by the sound of their names: older men named Rulon, Larue, or Lavell; older women named LaVera. Some of us named Brigham or Spencer for modern prophets, and some of us named Moroni, Mahonri, Nephi, or Jared for Book of Mormon ones. Some even had well-known Mormon last names like Allred, Hatch, Rigby, Ricks, Tanner, Cannon, and Young.

We knew we all followed the same code of rules. Not only the easy and obvious ones, such as no murder, no lying, no stealing, no taking the name of the Lord in vain, of course, but subtler ones handed down by our prophets in Salt Lake City. No playing with face cards. No masks, even on Halloween. No two-piece bathing suits. No dating a non-Mormon; no dating before age sixteen. No R-rated movies. For Mormon women: no working outside the home. No work, sports, shopping, swimming, or television on Sunday. Keep a personal journal. Grow a vegetable garden. Keep a year's supply of food in your garage. Hold special family worship meetings every Monday night. Read the scriptures every day. Pray morning and night. Pray always.

How we loved to see one another, we Mormons, out and about in the confusion of the greater world we traversed each day, undetectable, to be able to grip one anothers' unstained hands with firm missionary handshakes and speak the familiar language of our people, a language of modern prophets and apostles, small Utah towns, church auxiliaries, missions and missionaries, words that smelled like laundry detergent, hymnals, and cottonwood trees, words as comforting as bread made from home-ground wheat and smothered with home-canned peach preserves. How we loved to see the family vans out on the highways of the Mormon corridor, steaming along the I-15, up past the old Mormon outpost at San Bernardino, through the old Mormon settlement of Las Vegas, through the red bluffs of St. George, Utah, up through the Great Basin to our family reunions and missionary farewells. A man in our ward named LaRue had a personalized California license plate that read "LDSRU12," LDS being the acronym for "Latter-day Saints," another name we Mormons called ourselves. How it felt to be LaRue, fielding friendly noncaffeinated honks and waves all day long from other Mormons, so happy to be Mormons, so happy to know and be known.

To the untrained eye, I knew I looked like any other third grader: with my dark brown hair in a Dorothy Hamill cut, brown freckles on the bridge of my nose, and wearing my favorite birthday pair of vinyl zip-up boots.

But every Sunday at church I learned that there was something powerful in my careful steps and clean language and shiny caffeine-free skin and hair, something that might catch the corner of someone's eye, leading them first to inquire about and then to discover for themselves the joy of Mormon living. "Dare to Be Different," was the motto the older kids recited in their Sunday meetings. "CTR" read the letters on the little green-enameled ring I got in the mail after sending my nickels and dimes to Salt Lake City, its letters reminding me to "Choose the Right" at all times, as I went about my daily life with the eyes of the world upon me.

Such was the power of our sparkling difference, I learned, that Brigham Young University had deputized a special precision Mormon youth song-and-dance team called the Young Ambassadors to spend all year circling the globe, enticing audiences to righteousness with their trademark wholesome show tunes and modest yet professional theatrical costumes.

Perhaps I was no Young Amabassador, at least *not yet*, but I often rehearsed scenarios, just for the sake of readiness:

I might be sitting at a marble-topped ice-cream-parlor table, patiently, beatifically waiting for my glass of root beer, while the children all around me—even the birthday girl herself—unthinkingly splashed their Coca-Colas.

I might be the only third grader who stayed behind to help the homely boy with leg braces ready himself for the playground.

"What makes you so different?" the yard duty in her orange safety pinafore, or the auburn-haired mother of the birthday girl might ask.

Or it might be many, many years later, and two young missionaries in white shirts might knock on the yard duty's door, or the door of the birthday girl, or the door of her now gray-haired mother, and recalling my shining goodness, they might keep the door open a little longer and agree to hear the story of Joseph Smith or even read the Book of Mormon. For all around us, as they taught us at Church, people were hungry for answers, hungry for the gospel to give order and purpose to their lives.

I saw it for myself, that hunger, in the filmstrips and movies my Sunday School teachers projected against the church's cool white cinder-block walls.

The favorite among us—me, Juli, Shayne, and the other boys and girls in Sunday School—was the movie called *Man's Search for Happiness.*

If we begged hard enough, we could convince our teachers to put down their Salt Lake City–printed lesson manuals and show it again and again: every time the same sequence of images, every time the same spiral of feelings winding up in my chest.

It opened with a blond man crossing a bridge over a leafy stream. The voice-over wonders, as he gazes at the wavering reflection of his impossibly chiseled face in the water: "Who am I? How did I come to be? Time: where does it take me? Toward death? And then what? Where did I come from?"

Surely, I felt, I was among the lucky ones in all the world to have beautiful answers to those questions, and I wanted so badly for the man gazing into the water to have them too.

The surface of the water rippled and then faded into swirls of turquoise, purple, and brown, inhabited by people in white clothing, moving peacefully and contentedly among the mists, none of them touching, but some of them talking softly in groups. "At birth you did not suddenly flare into existence out of nowhere," the confident voice related. "You have always lived. In pre-earth life you lived with your Heavenly Father as his spirit sons and daughters. You learned, until you were ready to come to earth."

My mind reached back against its opaque limits, against the forgetting we called the "veil," stretching for a glimpse of some corner of that pre-earthly life.

Suddenly the screen split: on one side, the swirly pre-earth realms, on the other, the cold hospital, the masked doctor and nurse holding a newborn baby by his heels. "Upon entering mortal life, the memory of your life before birth was blotted out, that you might live by faith and further prepare for everlastingness," the voice continued.

I reached and remembered nothing but still felt the certainty of my own life, my spirit, like a long blue cotton thread from one of the spools in my grandmother's sewing box, but without beginning or end.

On the screen, the operating room melted into the unholy laugh of a nodding mechanical clown, the gateway arch of a carnival on a darkened studio lot. "Life offers you two precious gifts: one is time, the other—freedom of choice. You are free to exchange your time for thrills."

The headlights of a roller-coaster car flared out of the darkness and rushed by. The darkness of the carnival is a menace.

"You may trade it for base desires."

The stockinged calves of four female dancers can-canned across the screen, red marabou boas floating along with them.

"You may invest it in greed."

A sideshow barker wearing shirtsleeve garters spun a roulette wheel and flashed tickets to the captive crowd.

"You may purchase with it vanity."

A man in a gray suit and fedora admired himself in a fun-house mirror, while his blond wife chortled gamely along.

"You may spend it in pursuit of material goods."

Another man raised an air rifle to his shoulder and took aim at the mechanical ducks going round and round in the shooting gallery. *Pop-pop-pop.* The sideshow barker handed the wife a china doll, which slipped through her fingers and fell to the ground, where it broke into pieces. She makes a sour sound of disappointment.

"But in these you will find no lasting satisfaction."

The woman gave her husband a disgusted look. How I disliked her, how I disliked the way she glared at her husband.

Who wanted a china doll, really? Was that all this earthlife had for me?

A series of ticking clocks converged on the screen.

"Every minute, every hour, every day of your mortal life must be accounted for. Your eternal reward will be according to your choosing."

The camera panned down the length of a grandfather clock, as a gray-haired grandfather in a suit and tie adjusted his own pocket watch and showed it to his blond grandson who was wearing a plaid vest.

How much better it must have felt to be in their warm bread-smelling house, I imagined, than it did in the dark carnival full of randomness and cheap prizes.

"After death, though your mortal body lies in the earth, you, your spirit self, will continue to live." The outline figure of a man steps up through a skyscape of amber and burgundy clouds.

"Like coming out of a darkened room into the light, through death you will reemerge into a place of reawakening and find loved ones waiting to welcome you."

And so it was revealed: the man was the gray-haired grandfather, who left behind his pocket watch and traded his gray suit for clothes all in white. He stepped out of the mists, arms raised, into the embrace of his gray-haired wife and countless others clad in all white who stepped forward out of the mists to welcome him, as the Mormon Tabernacle Choir sang exultant.

Seeing their embrace, I thought always of my own white-haired Utah-born grandmother, still alive, but thirty miles down the freeway. It always felt like a million miles, and I wanted to be sitting at her kitchen table. I wanted her to slice me a dish of peaches. I wanted to feel the soft worn pads of her thumbs in my hands. I wanted to sit on the back porch wrapped in an afghan on my grandfather's lap watching the planes line up in the night sky to land at Los Angeles International Airport, coming home.

"This is the way to peace, happiness, and eternal life," the voice concluded, as the scene changed from heaven to a concourse of living mortals, pressing forward, some in the traditional costumes of their native countries, Swiss, Samoan, American Indian, babies in their arms.

"Hold fast to that which is good. Only if you are unafraid of truth will you find it. It leads to limitless opportunities, with your loved ones with you, always and forever. Therein lies your happiness. A happiness deeper than passing pleasures. A happiness not of the moment, but of eternity."

I felt the voices of the Mormon Tabernacle Choir surging all around me, and I thought of the broken china doll on the ground, and the sour look on the face of the vain and disappointed woman. Every time I saw *Man's Search for Happiness* I promised myself: I would be different. For what were they to me, the passing pleasures of this life—profanity, face cards, and Coca-Cola, even my favorite birthday zip-up vinyl boots—the hollow pleasures of the spooky carnival of earthlife? What were any of these next to the knowledge of who I was, where I came from, and where I was going? In the cool safety of the darkened Sunday School room, I hugged my knees and felt the pull of a great, deep longing through the center of my chest. Where else would I rather be than in the embrace of my ancestors on the other side of the veil?

On Friday nights, after my mother had put my younger sisters and brother to sleep, I was allowed to stay up and watch the Donny and Marie Osmond show on the ABC television network on the little television in my parents' upstairs bedroom.

How proud I felt of them, the world's most famous Mormons, their noncaffeinated smiles sparkling out on invisible television rays from Osmond Studios in Orem, Utah, radiating across the globe, causing untold throngs of unsuspecting television viewers across the globe to rub their eyes in wonder and ask themselves, "What is it that makes them different?" and maybe even "Who am I? Where did I come from? Where am I going?" Even better was knowing that I was part of a special audience of other Mormons around the globe who all tuned in these Friday nights to watch with special intention the opening ice-skating number with glamorous skaters in spandex and sequins, the "I'm a Little Bit Country, I'm a Little Bit Rock and Roll" duets, the wholesome comedy skits, the outrageous costume changes, delicious down to the closing song, the deeply true brown eyes of Donny and Marie connecting directly with ours:

*May tomorrow be a perfect day,*
*May you find love and laughter along the way.*
*May God keep you in His tender care,*
*Till He brings us together again.*
*Good night everybody!*

Sitting on the avocado-green shag carpet in front of the television screen, I felt a deep connection to the thousands of other Osmond-watching Mormons: all of us knew who we were, where we came from, and where we were going! And we also knew that, unbeknownst to millions of unsuspecting non-Mormon viewers worldwide, the "God" Donny and Marie were thinking about when they sang their farewell song was *our* God, the same God who appeared to Joseph Smith in the Sacred Grove, the God for whom our ancestors crossed the plains, the God who commanded us to keep our bodies clean by abstaining from Coca-Cola. On Friday nights I knew that even though I did not live in Utah, I was not alone. There was Marie, and across the country, there were other girls like me watching her, she being the best possible version of our homely Mormon selves. *We Mormons: we were everywhere the satellites touched.*

How to describe what I felt in that instant, when Marie winked at the camera just for *us* through her thick black fake eyelashes? How to describe the burgundy and turquoise watercolor tones of the pre-existence and afterlife, the joy I felt hearing the surging sounds of the Mormon Tabernacle, and seeing peoples of every nation, kindred, and tongue stepping forward into the currents of eternity? How to describe my hunger for that beautiful world of sparkling difference beyond profanity, and beyond the pollution we learned about in school, and beyond the fearsome men, who, according to our parents and teachers, might lure us into their cars with candy? How to describe the hunger that made me climb up in my mother's lap and cry for its pleasure and beauty?

When I was eight years old, I could not yet see the shadows in my world of sparkling difference, the hard edges of the lines we drew to distinguish ourselves from others. I did not know, for example, that the people I loved had only recently allowed black men to hold the priesthood, after excluding them for more than a century. I did not even know how to see that there were no black people sitting in our pews on Sunday, just as I did not know how to see that there were no black children in my elementary school. After all, my grandparents and parents had moved away from Los Angeles to the orange grove suburbs to put freeway miles between themselves and places like Compton and Watts. In my primary classes, I learned stories of the kind and loving Jesus who would return to save us all from the destruction and cruelty of the earthly world. How was I to know that Mormons had played our own special if minor role in that cruelty?

Yet all around me, just within the range of my hearing, grown-ups spun elaborate stories to explain away the absence of black people in the Mormon world. Some said that African Americans were descended from Cain, who killed Abel, or, as my mother explained, from Ham, the son who humiliated Noah. It was the curses God levied on those ancient characters that had been transmitted and preserved through time in the blackness of black people, and it was the curse of blackness that barred black people from the priesthood. Perhaps it was my father who told me another version of the story: that in the life before this one, our souls sat in great councils and deliberated over God's plan to send us to this earth, where we would learn and grow through a lifetime of experience. Debates led to conflict, and in these great conflicts in heaven, it was said, the souls of those who did not fight valiantly for God's plan later came to earth in the bodies of black people. The people I loved dropped heavy tears over stories of our pioneer ancestors trapped by snowstorms in the Rocky Mountains and yet did not blink when they stated with assurance that millions upon millions of African people across time were permanently unworthy of God's favor. All of this I silently absorbed.

It would be many years before I learned to sort out the stories that had been sown into me like tares amidst the wheat. I did not yet know and would not know for many years that even when I was a child there were in Salt Lake City Mormon historians who had found evidence that in the early days of the Church black Mormons had truly belonged just like the rest of us, that there had been black Mormon men whose hands had blessed and baptized and anointed. And I did not yet know and would not know for many years that priesthood had been yanked away from black men and a host of excuses allowed to grow up and take the place of doctrine.

These are the unspoken legacies we inherit when we belong to a people: not only luminous visions of eternal expanses of loving-kindness, but actual human histories of exclusion and rank prejudice. We inherit not only the glorious histories of our ancestors, but their human failings too, their kindness, their tenderness, and their satisfaction with easy contradictions; their wisdom as well as their ignorance, arrogance, and presumption, as our own. We inherit all the ways in which our ancestors and parents and teachers were wrong, as well as the ways they were right: their sparkling differences, and their human failings. There is no unmixing the two.

# 3

# signs of the times

During the Reagan years of the Cold War, my mother and I would watch jets and helicopters traverse the skies over the orange groves behind our house.

Standing by the swimming pool, my mother pointed out all the strategic targets within a few miles of our house: Marine Corps Air Station El Toro, south across the orange groves; John Wayne Airport to the west, across the asparagus and strawberry fields; and two massive concrete blimp hangars at the Marine Corps Air Station Tustin.

"They'll drop the bombs right on top of us," she said, her eyes on the horizon.

"We'll be fine. We'll be gone in the twinkling of an eye."

A green Marine CH-46 helicopter made its way down eucalyptus-lined Peters Canyon toward the Pacific Ocean. Tandem rotors whirred.

"No radiation sickness for us. No losing teeth and hair. No starving out the nuclear winter," my mother continued.

"We're the lucky ones," she told herself, then turned and headed back into the house.

I was eleven years old. A Mormon girl living, as we did in those days, at the convergence of so many great and terrible narratives. Cold War arms race. Domino theory. Star Wars missile defense systems. Last days. President Ronald Reagan was the white-cowboy-hat hero of our end-times dreams, a rugged horseman of the apocalypse who rode out from the West to save our divinely inspired Constitution from the dangers of one-world government, Communism, taxes, and other godless destruction. And we Mormons, we who had once been a renegade prophetic sect driven by mobs into the deserts beyond the United States, had undergone a wondrous transformation into the finest patriot partisans of the end-times. How to reconcile it? I did not know. All I knew was that, somehow, history was swinging our way, the way the prophets had always predicted, toward the great destruction that would bring the opening of the skies and the return of a beautiful Jesus, with healing in his wings. On the refrigerator in the kitchen hung a full color print of that moment: Jesus in his blue-tinged robes, a pink sash around his waist, arms open, troops of heavenly hosts raising their trumpets on either side, the heavens themselves parting, a breach in the fabric of time.

• • •

My mother and father prepared our family for that final moment, as well as for more everyday Southern California catastrophes—earthquake, riot, fire—in the most practical of ways. First, all six of us—my mother, father, brother, sisters, and me—had blue canvas backpacks equipped with seventy-two hours' worth of the necessities of life:

a change of clothes
five packets of nuts and raisins
one silver space blanket
three freeze-dried food bars
two water bottles
a poncho
a tiny first-aid kit
a candle
matches
a bright-orange plastic flashlight

Second, industrial-size water barrels lined the back of our house. This was in case a nuclear attack or ash falling from the skies made the swimming pool unfit to drink. Cupboards in the garage were stocked, on direction from church leaders, with a year's supply of food for us all: giant tin drums of hard red wheat kernels, textured vegetable protein, powdered milk, potato pearls, pinto beans, dried apples, and cooking oil.

Third, every year the members of our Mormon congregation held drills to practice what we might do in case of catastrophe. We walked the house-to-house routes we would use to check on one another. At church, even eleven- and twelve-year-old girls like me learned the bare skills of survival: how to build fires, lash tables from tree branches, and perform advanced first aid. "Keep lots of trash bags around," said Sister Tucker at one of our Tuesday afternoon youth meetings. "You may need them for latrines, or to dispose of dead bodies." Another Tuesday afternoon, she taught us how to tie off a severed artery. "Just reach in, find the one that's spurting, and tie a knot in it," she said.

We prepared for the end-times mentally and spiritually as well. I studied the picture of Jesus's second coming on the refrigerator, slowly accustoming myself to the idea of a breach in time, surprised by the relief the idea afforded me. My family prayed together every night, fasted once a month, and read our scriptures, a discipline that would sustain us through any disaster and ready us to receive the promptings of the Spirit that would guide us all to safety. In Sunday School we rehearsed the lists of signs of the times compiled from the words of the prophet Isaiah, John the Revelator, Book of Mormon prophets, and our own local homegrown experts, balding, heavyset men who worked as aerospace engineers during the week, led Boy Scout outings on Saturdays, and studied Egyptology in their home offices on Sundays after church. These signs of the times were:

Wars and rumors of wars.
Earthquakes in diverse places.
The desert blossoming as a rose.
The teaching of organic evolution in public schools.
The construction of a great highway from the north.
The organization of the United Nations.
Bar codes on everything.
Drought.
Fires.
Famine.
Pestilence.
Strikes, anarchy, and violence.
Love waxing cold.
False prophets and anti-Christs.
The gospel being preached in every nation, to every
kindred, and in every tongue.
The literal gathering of the twelve tribes of Israel from
their hiding places around the globe.
The killing of two missionaries or prophets in
Jerusalem, their bodies left to rot in the streets for
two days.
The building of the New Jerusalem in Missouri.
The endangerment of the Constitution of the United
States, which would hang by a thread, to be
rescued by righteous Mormons.
The ancient archenemy forces of Gog and Magog
threatening the destruction of Israel.

A war of Armageddon.
The continents coming back together into one land mass.

My parents read the writings of experts like W. Cleon Skousen, staunch anti-Communist patrolman of the Mormon corridor, whose books lined the shelves of our Orange County ranch houses: *The Naked Communist*, *The Naked Capitalist*, *The Making of America*, *The Miracle of America*, *The First 2,000 Years*, *The Third Thousand Years*, *The Fourth Thousand Years*, *Prophecy and Modern Times*.

Back in 1963, Skousen sniffed out the secret goals of the Communists in our midst and compiled a list of warning signs published in anti-Communist bulletins from Florida to California. These warning signs of Communist infiltration included:

Diplomatic negotiations with enemy nuclear regimes.
Nuclear disarmament, or the promotion of nuclear disarmament.
Free trade between all nations.
American aid to all nations.
Recognition of Red China.
Abolition of US loyalty oaths.
Liberal control of school boards and curriculums.
Liberal control of newspapers, radio, television, and movies.

Communist-plant artists and teachers celebrating
ugliness everywhere.
Elimination of prayer in schools.
Criticism of the Constitution and Founding Fathers.
Pornography, homosexuality, divorce, atheism,
secularism, and psychiatry.

On the clay hills of Orange County, we studied and watched and prayed for the smoke plumes of the end-times to rise. What a thrill of relief I felt in the fall of my eleventh year, when the Santa Ana winds blew jets of fire down our dry canyons and the skies turned red, and we loaded our family photographs and books of genealogy into the station wagon and prepared to drive away. As the line of wildfire approached, burning through the eucalyptus groves, I monitored my insides. Terror, panic, tears, the urge to seek comfort from parents—these I observed and then canceled, proud of my emotional preparedness. In these moments, I soberly reasoned, there was no room for such extravagance.

There were a few signs of the times, signs of creeping moral decay undermining the social fabric of the divinely designed American nuclear family, that Cleon Skousen did not foresee. There was, for example, Phil Donahue, who wedged himself and his prodding microphone into Southern California network television in the early 1980s, his coming forewhispered by my mother and other stalwarts against unwholesome television programming like *Three's Company* and other screenfuls of cohabitational jiggling blondes that a simple turn of the dial might admit into our living rooms. Nor did Cleon Skousen foresee the national campaign for the Equal Rights Amendment, to which the Mormon Church declared its formal public opposition.

When my teacher Mrs. Stick assigned our sixth-grade term paper, I immediately chose the ERA as my research topic. Finding nothing about the amendment on the shelves of my school library, I asked my mother for help. On the kitchen table, she laid out a rainbow arc of glossy pamphlets: the Mormon Church's official briefing on *The Church and the Proposed Equal Rights Amendment: A Moral Issue*, mailed to every Mormon home, as well as slick little American-flag festooned brochures produced by Phyllis Schlafly, the carefully coiffured blond matriarch founder of the anti-Communist, pro-family Eagle Forum. I studied the pamphlets closely. From them, I learned that if the United States of America adopted into its Constitution the statement that "equality of rights under the law shall not be denied or abridged by the United States or by any State on account of sex," these words would in fact not correct long-standing gender inequities but rather endanger our families, demean the special and sacred roles of women, and harm the nation. Married women and mothers would be drafted into the military. Courts would no longer require men to provide for their wives and children.

More women would become lesbians. And, worst of all, the new law might institute unisex bathrooms.

"Of course we don't oppose equal rights for women," my mother explained, precise and articulate as she placed a block of frozen ground beef in the microwave oven. "It's just that the Equal Rights Amendment is the wrong way to go about it."

Sitting at the kitchen table, a stack of blank notebook paper before me, with the chunk of frozen beef spinning, warming, and graying in the microwave, I listened and took careful notes. *Unisex bathrooms?* I tried not to imagine the giant shoes in the next stall, the sight of men's backsides as they faced the wall holding their private parts: not the innocuous pink digit I had seen when I changed my baby brother's diaper, but the unimaginable member of the adult male body. In what moral universe, I wondered, was the sight of a strange man's penis a moral or political good?

Surely, if there were a sign of the times, unisex bathrooms could be it.

The summer after sixth grade I attended a special summer camp for girls at Brigham Young University, where, in addition to taking classes in scripture study, scrapbooking, and modest fashions, we gathered every morning in our Sunday dresses in great air-conditioned lecture halls to hear speeches from the men who made a living teaching Church-sponsored seminary classes in Utah public schools.

Driving wood-paneled station wagons and wearing dark polyester suits, they came to point out all the wickedness and worldliness that threatened to engulf us on every side. They told us that we were a powerful generation, living in the sixth millennium since the earth's creation, the Saturday of time, Sunday being the seventh millennium, the second coming of Jesus Christ. They promised that we ourselves would do battle with Satanic hosts, and some described their own experiences in the mission field. Like spiritual linebackers, they were, to hear them tell the stories, clashing with and blocking unseen powers of darkness.

One teacher named Brother Christianson specialized in the dangers of popular music, an urgent hazard facing us youth of the latter days. He told us that Satan specialized in presenting bad things in the guise of good things, transfiguring himself into an angel of light, just to deceive and confuse us. To illustrate his point, he related a local Utah high school legend: how some cheerleaders had once tricked haughty but unsuspecting basketball players into what they thought was a caramel-apple-eating contest at a pep rally; not until they had wolfed down half the "apples" did the players realize they were actually eating caramel-covered onions. That's how Satan works too, Brother Christianson said: the caramel is music, one of the sweetest mediums on earth, but instead of wrapping it around wholesome, inspiriting goodness, Satan wraps it around the stink of pure evil. Cunning as a vengeful cheerleader, he is, that old Satan.

Brother Christianson told us that the music our shaggy-haired seventeen-year-old cousins listened to—Led Zeppelin, the Eagles, Styx, Electric Light Orchestra—had Satanic messages specially ironed onto its sonic backsides. He wheeled out a giant reel-to-reel tape player, and we all leaned forward in our seats in the BYU auditorium to hear Robert Plant make gurgling sounds Brother Christianson decoded for us as "Here's to my sweet Satan."

When Brother Christianson finished, we left the air-conditioned lecture halls and wandered out into the bright ninety-degree summer afternoons, changed from our Sunday dresses into modest one-piece swimsuits, and walked to the dormitory pools, or bought ice cream from the BYU agriculture department creamery. Grasshoppers gnashed their heads against the cinder-block walls and yellow grasses. Redheaded boys from nearby farm towns, wearing ropers and Wrangler jeans, waited around outside the lobby daring themselves to strike up a conversation with out-of-town girls. A few blocks away at the Missionary Training Center, a pageant of farm families and city families boiled over with tears as they, one after another, kissed their nineteen-year-old missionary sons good-bye for two years.

At night the nineteen-year-old missionaries in training memorized lessons in Spanish, Japanese, Portugese, and

Italian, preparing to fulfill the prophecy that in the last days the gospel would be taught in every nation, to every kindred, and in every tongue. Meanwhile, up in the high-rise Deseret Towers dormitories, Laura and Doreen, my new summer camp girlfriends from small Mormon towns in Wyoming and Nevada, and I lay down on our narrow dormitory beds in our cotton flannel pajamas. Outside the window, the golden spires of the Provo Temple shone brightly against the shale-covered Wasatch Foothills.

Gazing up at the acoustic tile ceilings, Laura, Doreen, and I talked about all that was afoot in these latter days:

> How the inexplicable little Procter & Gamble insignia—a crescent man-in-the-moon face and stars—was in fact a Satanic emblem, with little "6 6 6"s curled up in his beard in the design.

> How according to the journals of nineteenth-century Mormon missionaries, Bigfoot is Cain, marked by a suit of dark fur for his crime against his brother, and condemned to forever wander the foothills of the intermountain West.

> How three faithful men from Book of Mormon times who were excused from death by Jesus himself are also, like Bigfoot-Cain, now wandering the backroads and byways of the intermountain West

in the guise of friendly hitchhikers who bail out
Mormon cars broken down in the heat or snow.

Growing giddy as the night grew late, Laura broke out in Disney torch songs adapted for the end-times: "Someday, my prince will come . . . in the *millennium*!"

I lay on my back and felt the cotton flannel on my flat chest. Could it be that we would not attain our maturity before the second coming of Christ? Could it be that the end would come before our first kiss, our first boyfriend? Could it be that a rent in the fabric of time would circumvent our destined confrontation with the unspeakable mysteries of the marriage bed, the reality of the adult male member? Could the end-times save us from that end? Might we be transmuted into the eternities unchanged, as chaste as we were in our flannel pajamas in the single-sex BYU dormitories, as chaste as ministering angels?

We could only hope.

A few months after I got home from summer camp at Brigham Young University, my cousin, Danny, a Judas Priest fan, shot himself between the eyes with a Saturday night special. He survived, the entire left side of his body crumpled inward and palsied, a living, limping monument to all the warnings and forewhisperings of our teachers and parents in these latter days.

• • •

*Saturday's Warrior* was the name of a Mormon musical that made the rounds of church houses across the American West during those last years of the Cold War. The play opened in the gauzy realms of pre-earthly life, with a family promising to look after one another on earth and help each other return safely home to heaven. The urgency of their promises were, of course, heightened by the fact that it was the Saturday of time, and many apostasy-inducing dangers afoot on the earth threatened the security of the family. In ward-house cultural halls all across the Mormon West, we saw ourselves, our families, onstage, and we sang:

*These are the few, the warriors*
*Saved for Saturday,*
*to come the last day of the world*
*These are they, on Saturday.*
*These are the strong, the warriors*
*Rising in their might*
*to win the battle raging in*
*the hearts of men, on Saturday.*

I dreamed one night that my father and I were running down the empty freeways of Orange County, California, up and down the overpasses, as the hills turned red with fire and dissolved into great pools of oil. "Oh," I turned and said to him in great relief, "isn't it wonderful that what is going on outside finally matches what is taking place inside the human heart?"

I was eleven. And what a gift it was, growing up in a world taut with conflict and luminous with meaning. Time was not empty; the days were not a sequence of identical rooms to be filled with whatever thin fantasies I myself might collect from television sitcoms and project upon the Sheetrock walls. No. Time was a vector of godly intention, the fractal plume of something expansive and infinite, and my purpose—and I knew it—to discern the patterns of its unfolding. We rehearsed and rehearsed and rehearsed the great stories of destruction, the fall of the ancient American civilizations of the Book of Mormon. In my illustrated edition the gray-haired prophet Mormon collapsed in exhaustion on a hill of slain Nephites, cradling the golden plates of the Book of Mormon in one arm, the other arm outstretched toward the red horizon, the wingspans of vultures arcing against the sky: "O, ye fair ones, how could ye have departed from the ways of the Lord?" We grew up always ready to abandon this world, to take our small backpacks of bottled water, freeze-dried food, first-aid kits, and candles, and simply walk away, walk as far as Missouri if we had to, if that was where the New Jerusalem would be built.

What comfort there was in going to sleep each night with a head full of first-aid tips, a three-day backpack in the bedroom closet, and down the hall a thousand pounds of wheat sealed up against doom. What a gift it was to be a girl nestled high and tight in the dormitories at Brigham Young University, while the missionaries in training chanted their lessons just a few hundred yards away and the couples in church clothes with little suitcases came to and went from the Provo Temple at all hours, steadily doing proxy baptisms and eternal marriages for dead United States presidents and regular everyday people. Like bees in a hive, we were all about our business—workers, receivers, and foragers—held together by the frequencies of our dance. What a gift it was to be taught to think of myself as a soldier. A warrior.

I belonged. I belonged. And if I did not belong, what would become of me? What mockery would time make of my small, freckled life? What of the dark aimlessness ebbing at the edges of my life, where Mormonism stopped and the world began? What if, like Danny, I got pulled under?

And where else, as a middle-class girl in the suburban American West, would I find anyone who dared to map an unfolding universe on a chalkboard, or hint that time itself might be capable of dilation and compression, as what was experienced as one day in heaven constituted more than a thousand years on earth? Who else could confirm my not altogether incorrect perception that there were powerful forces at work that I myself had little hope of directing, and yet might somehow survive? Who else would teach me how to do the actual work of surviving?

It is September 1, 1983. I am almost twelve years old. We

are folding laundry in front of *Days of Our Lives* on the little television set in my mother's bedroom. Suddenly a somber-faced Tom Brokaw appears onscreen, with an illustration of a plane hovering over his left shoulder. He announces that Korean Air Lines Flight 007 has just been shot down by Soviet jet fighters over the Sea of Japan.

"Oh!" my mother exclaims, bolting upright, her eyes fixed on Tom Brokaw.

My younger sister looks to me to explain.

"Mom?"

"Shhhhh! It's the Soviets!" she hisses. Her voice is electric with thrill. "This could be it! This could be the end!"

# 4

# marie osmond's guide to beauty, health & style

The year we all turned twelve, the boys in my Sunday School class received the priesthood: the spiritual authority to lead, bless, and baptize, passed from Mormon father to Mormon son by the laying on of hands.

That's what Chuckie, Mike, and Brian got for their twelfth birthdays.

I got *Marie Osmond's Guide to Beauty, Health & Style.*

Which is not to say I would have ever traded.

No, I needed Marie. I needed her sparkly clear television voice to guide me through the daunting mysteries of *Beauty, Health & Style* and initiate me into my young womanhood.

She was, after all, someone I could really trust. A Mormon girl, for starters—and better yet, a rare kind of Mormon girl, just like me, with dark hair and a twinkle of definite ambition in her eye. Marie's head was full of pioneer histories, end-times prophecies, and hymns, just like mine. Like me, she had probably already puzzled over the problem of polygamy: since you had to be married to get into the celestial kingdom, the highest level of our Mormon heaven, and it was obvious to all concerned that righteous women outnumbered righteous men, might God and our husbands ask us to accept a second wife for the eternities? And which would be worse, to share a husband, or keep another woman out of heaven? No doubt, Marie was still puzzling over that one, as I was. But unlike me, Marie had already mastered the intricacies of *Beauty, Health & Style.* Who else could give me up-to-date but faith-tested insider information on "turning 12 clothing separates into 3 dozen outfits," "ten hair do's and don'ts," "complexion routines for four kinds of skin," and my "three makeup personalities." Marie was not only set on getting to the celestial kingdom, the highest level of our Mormon heaven, but on arriving there without split ends or blemishes, with just the right makeup personality, wearing a precisely placed beauty mark and an impeccable apricot-colored crepe de chine shirtwaist dress, or a cream cowl-neck sweater and forest-green corduroy skirt, or a yellow jacquard tunic.

I pored over the pictures in *Marie Osmond's Guide to Beauty, Health & Style,* gorgeous publicity stills shot on location in and around *Provo, Utah!* home of Brigham Young University, and the city of my destiny. First, there was long-haired, chubby thirteen-year-old Marie in a white evening dress with Donny in a matching white-quilted tuxedo vest, and both of them flashing their trademark smiles on the Osmond holiday television special. I flipped the pages forward. There I saw a transformed short-haired skinny seventeen-year-old Marie eating a takeout salad in her dressing room at Osmond Studios. And a few pages later, there was college-student Marie in a velour jogging suit, running, chin up, down a leafy lane in *Provo, Utah!* Marie, in full makeup, hair slicked back into a chic chignon, kneeling on the floor of her mother Olive's sewing room, nibbling on a perfectly manicured index finger while puzzling over the instructions on a dress pattern. Marie strolling across the Brigham Young University campus with two friends, smiling, all wearing unconstructed blazers, bootleg jeans, and stacked heel boots, their arms full of notebooks. Marie and her same two friends in jeans and sweatshirts playing a flirty but chaste coed game of touch football on the dormitory lawn, then petite Marie getting "tackled" by three hunky guys (one shirtless, none of them Osmond brothers) in the same flirty but chaste coed game of touch football. Marie and BYU roommates piecing a quilt. Marie looking pensive on the stairs outside the BYU Wilkinson Center, wearing a button-down plaid shirt and a pair of home-sewn jeans with a custom MARIE OSMOND label on the back pocket.

All these Maries I studied carefully. Memorized their poses. Longed for a manicured nail to nibble on, or a velour jogging suit, or a pair of jeans with a custom MARIE OSMOND label on the back pocket, or best of all, a touch football game on the dormitory lawn at BYU.

And though I was only twelve and years away from *Provo, Utah!* I resolved that I was not too young to begin to make myself into the woman I hoped to be. And for this, *Marie Osmond's Guide to Beauty, Health & Style* was my instruction manual.

The *Guide* contained a repertoire of routines essential to my personal transformation. First things first, I should scrutinize my skin in the bathroom mirror to determine whether it was *normal*, *dry*, *oily*, or *combination*. Each type had its own set of rules, its own morning and evening routines, even its own special homemade facial recipe, to apply once a week. For combination skin like mine, the key—Marie said—was to strive for "balance" between the dry spots around my cheek and eyes and the oiliness of my dreaded "T-Zone." The dry spots I should lavish with gentle cleansers, splash lightly with warm water, and dab with moisturizing lotions, *using circular, upward motions only* to preserve skin tone and texture. The T-Zone, however, called for an alcohol-based astringent to bring my active oil glands into line. The weekly facial would help too, especially if I steamed my face over a basin of boiling water, applied Marie's special mixture of oatmeal, honey, egg, and water to exfoliate, soothe, and tighten all at once, rinsing with cold water to close my pores.

Of course, having combination skin also required general lifestyle considerations to minimize break outs, such as drinking several large glasses of water every day to cleanse my system, eating fresh fruits and vegetables, and getting enough rest to combat stress and fatigue, which would only aggravate my worrisome oil glands. Exercise was important too. The *Guide* said that dance rehearsals at Osmond Studios every week kept Marie fit and slender, as did the occasional game of touch football with her eight Osmond brothers. Since I had neither a studio nor eight brothers, perhaps, I could make an especially enthusiastic effort during seventh-grade gym class, or ride my bike home from school. (As long as I had my inhaler with me.) If I did, within just a few weeks, Marie promised, I would look better and feel healthier. I resolved to take her at her word.

I also studied carefully Marie's list of prescribed cosmetics, applicators, and other beauty tools, and dreamed of the day I might assemble them all neatly organized in a compartmental lucite tray on a sheet of perfumed paper in the bathroom drawer now full of my uncleaned hairbrushes, my orthodontic appliance cases, and wads of dark hair my seven-year-old brother had pulled from my head. Marie's book laid out long lists of cosmetics: foundations, concealers, powders, eyeliners, eye pencils, caked eye shadows, cream blushes, mascaras, lip glosses, lipsticks, and lip pencils. Plus mustache wax to train wild brow hairs. Plus petroleum jelly to moisturize the eyelashes. There were also long sets of tools and applicators: sable brushes in three different shapes for the eyes, sable brushes in two different volumes for blush and powder, makeup sponges, cotton swabs, cotton balls, tweezers, false lashes, and an eyelash curler. I had never considered curling my eyelashes. I thought of the black-caked metal contraption that I saw in the bathroom drawer at my friend Missy's house (it belonged to her sister, a Mötley Crüe fan) and understood immediately why Marie urged us to clean our eyelash curlers once a week! There would be no black-caked eyelash curlers in my perfume-scented drawer!

I counted down the lists, totaling the number of items in my head. Thirty-one all together. Thirty-four, if you included a few color options among the eye shadows. Thirty-five, if you included a *nighttime* lipstick shade to alternate with the regular *daytime* color. My only source of income as a twelve-year-old was birthday gifts from my grandmother and odd babysitting jobs. There was a Mormon family in the neighborhood who would hire me to watch their two toddlers once a month so that they could make a visit to the Mormon temple in Los Angeles. On a good babysitting night—after paying my tithing—I could make almost $10. In a year, I calculated, if I worked hard and saved carefully in the glass jar under my bed, I could really begin to chip away at Marie's list of cosmetic essentials. I might even be able to afford an eyelash curler. That is, if I could convince my mom to load my brother and sisters into the station wagon and take me down to the Drug Emporium.

But maybe moderation was a good thing. Taking it slow was really okay. After all, I learned from the *Guide* that all eight Osmond brothers agreed that nothing looked worse on a young girl than globs of makeup. Marie picked up most of her cosmetics know-how at Osmond Studios from world-famous celebrity makeup artist Way Bandy, one-time makeup director for Charles of the Ritz, who had "designed" her makeup personality three separate times. She also did some experimentation with her cameraman Bob to see what appealed to the cameras. Since I did not know a world-famous celebrity makeup artist or have a cameraman, Marie suggested that I set aside an hour or two on Saturdays to investigate the latest tips and techniques in fashion magazines. If only I could get some.

Everyone is different, Marie assured me. On some girls, colored eye shadow might open their eyes, while on others colored eye shadow would certainly close them, and those girls should instead use a hint of blush under the eyebrows. *Perhaps I was one of them?* What mattered most was that I experimented and selected and applied my eye makeup with care, minding whether or not my eyes were close-set or wide-set, too small or too large, and remembering to take care of my eyes when they were overtired and puffy. Marie confided that she once accidentally discovered that the tannic acid in tea bags was good for puffy eyes. It sure must have been an accident, a good Mormon girl having caffeinated tea bags in her dressing room. Perhaps they belonged to Bob the cameraman or world-famous celebrity makeup artist Way Bandy.

For her hair, Marie turned to world-famous celebrity hair stylist Yusuke Suga, the Japanese-born inventor of the Dorothy Hamill wedge, master of his own salon at Bergdorf Goodman in New York City, stylist to Bianca Jagger, Gloria Vanderbilt, Cher, and Cheryl Tiegs. It was Suga whom Marie trusted to carve away her long, dark thirteen-year-old locks, unveiling then the tiny frame, strong cheekbones, and trademark Osmond smile loved by Gentiles the world over. Losing her long hair was, Marie confided, something of a shock at first, but she grew to value the versatility afforded by her new style.

I weighed her words, studying in the bathroom mirror my own shaggy shoulder-length style, a grown-out junior-high not-quite Farrah Fawcett. I wondered if a shorter style might be right for me too. I could never determine exactly whether my face was an *oval*, *square*, *heart-shaped*, or *round*. But the *Guide* did suggest that with my *small frame* and *small features*, a long style might be overpowering.

A few weeks later, when Becky the neighborhood haircut lady set up shop in our kitchen and all the Mormon families in the neighborhood sent their kids over for bang trims and bowl cuts, I decided to take a chance. I asked for a short new style, straight at the nape, with a permanent crown of curls on top. A hairdo just like the one in the photograph of Marie looking pensive in her private-label jeans outside the Brigham Young University student center in *Provo, Utah!*

Becky smiled and chatted excitedly with my mom. The chemicals burned at my nape and nostrils. The rollers were removed, my head rinsed in the kitchen sink, my hair cut and dried. Becky passed me her handheld mirror. What I beheld was not the hair of Marie, but a style rather like my own mother's. I felt a pit in my belly. I felt the miles between me and *Provo, Utah!* grow longer, and more impossible. But then I composed myself. In time—just like Marie—I too would grow to value the versatility of my short new style. Given time, I would get there.

My next step was to adopt Marie's own 62-minute schedule as my own early morning routine. Before I went to bed, I studied its seventeen numbered and precisely timed steps, from calisthenics (10 minutes) to eyedrops (1 minute) to hairstyle (4 minutes) to wardrobe (4 minutes) and breakfast (10 minutes). I had never timed my morning routine before, but it rarely took more than 20 minutes from the time I left my bed until the time I reached the kitchen for breakfast: 62 minutes! I absorbed the challenge of the routine and relished its transformative promise, then placed the book on the nightstand, pulled up my covers, said my prayers, and closed my eyes.

The clock radio went off at *6:00 a.m.* I turned it off, then reached for my *Marie Osmond's Guide to Beauty, Health*

*& Style.* First came calisthenics. Propping the guide up on my windowsill so I could see the pictures, I planted my feet 18 inches apart, stretched out my arms, and flattened my palms. Fifteen circles forward, fifteen circles backward. Palms up! Repeat! I glanced at the clock: *6:02 a.m.* I turned my eyes back to the penciled sketch of the lithe, long-haired girl in a belted workout ensemble. She appeared to be wearing blush, even though makeup was step seven. I raised my arms over my head and leaned left and right four times, keeping my palms turned inward. Palms in! Repeat! *6:03 a.m.* On schedule. I dropped to the brown carpeting for push-ups. The girl in the picture did hers plank-straight, her brushed hair falling neatly over one shoulder. Two or three plank-straight push-ups, this I could do, before surrendering to my knees. *Soon*, I thought, looking at the girl on the page. *Soon enough.* Fifteen push-ups. Repeat! *6:05 a.m.* My twelve-year-old body, so confusing to me in its extended lurch between childhood and puberty, felt good and clean and purposeful when I was lying on the brown carpet in my bedroom, doing my Marie calisthenics by the early-morning light of the bedside clock radio.

I paused, then flipped forward through the pages. There were eight exercises left: three kinds of leg lifts, two kinds of sit-ups. With only five minutes left in this segment of the schedule, I resolved to double my pace. It was *6:12 a.m.* by the time I completed two sets of the final exercise, the "windmill," which, Marie promised, would strengthen and lengthen my waist. Since I stood 4'10", lengthening seemed an especially welcome outcome. I directed a final glance toward the lithe, long-haired girl on the page, her brushed hair sweeping the ground as she completed the exercise. *6:13 a.m.* I tried not to worry about the lost three minutes as I carried the book into the bathroom. Perhaps I could win some time back by brushing my teeth in ninety seconds and skipping the mouthwash—there was none in the bathroom cabinet—or by dialing back my shower from five minutes to four. I stood under the shower spray, making calculations and mental adjustments. I could just omit step nine, "touch-up nail polish," since my nails were bitten too short to polish, or step ten, "remove hot rollers," given my now permanent crown of curls. I stepped out of the shower, wrapped a towel about my flat chest and narrow hips, towel-dried my hair, and turned to the makeup section of the *Guide.* Surely I would save time here too, given the fact that I owned only five of the thirty-one makeup essentials. I laid the book flat on the bathroom counter and glanced at it for guidance as I dabbed a chalky yellowish tube of concealer on a pimple, rimmed my eyes with a blue eyeliner pencil, and used a tiny synthetic brush to bring some color to my cheeks. I ran my eyes over Marie's two-page essay on blush and rouge, then scrutinized the pictures of Marie with her long-handled sable-hair blush brush and tried to follow her motions, starting at the apples of the cheeks and moving upward toward my temples. I stood back and looked at my image in the mirror under fluorescent lights. Did I look like "I'd taken a long walk in the country," as Marie recommended, or like I was wearing "war paint"? Did the pinkish-rusty shade of my blush harmonize with the electric blue of the eyeliner? No matter—it was *6:43 a.m.* Time to get dressed.

Turning next to the Style section of the *Guide*, I set out to discern my fashion personality. Was I was "the country girl" who likes casual, sporty clothes or a "very feminine young lady" who likes frills and lace, or "the sophisticated type," the trend-setter in the latest fashions? No, I sensed, reaching deep inside myself, I was none of these, but rather like Marie herself, someone who aimed to be not trendy but rather classy and chic, someone who liked "simple lines" without looking "matronly."

In order to build the wardrobe of my dreams, I would need to start from the basics, conducting first a searching inventory of my current holdings. Marie had included in the *Guide* a six-column inventory grid. Each column was labeled with its own genre of clothing: blouses, shirts, sweaters, jackets, pants, and skirts. But where in this grid, I wondered, should I catalog the plaid-wool Bermuda shorts my grandmother and I sewed especially for the first day of seventh grade? Counting through my worn Levi's and striped T-shirts, the immensity of the wardrobe project began to envelop me. I soon saw so many holes in my wardrobe grid, so many "wardrobe basics" missing.

I had none of the twelve essential components—the trousers and dress pants, the tailored shirts and blouses, the shirt-jacket, the velvet blazer—that Marie assured me constituted the foundation of any wardrobe and which would take me in their infinite variations, seamlessly, through the seasons, from winter to spring and fall. Her list itself only opened so many more questions: What was crepe de chine, and did they make trousers from that fabric in a children's size 12? Given my *small frame*, could I really carry off a shirt jacket? Or a blouson? Perhaps not, given my *short neck* and *small bust*, for which the *Guide* prescribed the flattering illusion of a boat-neck sweater. And although (being intellectually mature for twelve years old) I appreciated the idea of a velvet blazer layered over a jersey-blend skirt, I could not figure out where I would wear such an outfit: to watch my sisters' games at the softball field (asthma kept me from playing)? to piano lessons? to hang out in the basketball gym at church? Without money of my own, without a driver's license, stranded in my suburban bedroom miles from the nearest retail store, all I could do was dream of a wardrobe like Marie's: "three dozen looks from one dozen fashion selections," an infinitely expansive grid blooming not only with wardrobe possibility but with the glamorous promise of a life so unlike my own.

I dreamed of a life in *Provo, Utah!* where I might wear the outfits she prescribed to their assigned activities. Wool trousers for *ice-skating with friends*. Velvet blazers to *important business appointments*. Challis skirts to *dinner dates*. Blouson—with a vest perhaps—to *a romantic occasion*. And though I had none of these, still, I did not allow despair to set in, for like Marie, I was a resourceful girl, the descendant of Mormon pioneers, who during winter times made bread from the roots of desert lilies, and did they ever complain? No. If I could get by on hardtack and tea boiled from chaparral, certainly I could scare up a few accessories around the house; for example, a knitted cap still in its gift box from the back of my mother's closet, or a floral challis scarf filched from her underwear drawer, or a silk flower to slip behind my ear and glamorize any outfit. Yes, I could make do.

But for me, the most cherished moments in the Marie Osmond *Guide* were those when through her perfectly wardrobed prose shone the outlines of the great secret we shared in common: our Mormonism, our candle burning brightly under the bushel of our bodies. For what was most important was asking ourselves, "Who am I?" and not being pressured to follow the in crowd and lose our precious individuality. To keep my individuality, Marie knowingly warned, I might have to stand apart from the crowd. I might be lonely for a while. *How did she know? I already was!* But with a little motivation and effort, I could develop my beauty and my "inner assets," by starting with the basics like hair and makeup, or even by developing a talent, like music, dance, or drama. And taking up a good hobby—for Marie, it was needlepoint—would help me clear my head when feelings of depression set in.

It was important, Marie said, to remember that so much of what I did or did not do during this special time in my life would impinge directly on my future. For example, math class—which we all knew girls were supposed to hate—would help me someday balance the family budget, and I would certainly rely on what I learned in Home Economics to care for my children and husband every day. So too what was important about diet and exercise was not only slimming and reducing, but remembering the future children we hoped to have some day. For this reason, we must not only do our morning calisthenics and eat our quick, nourishing breakfasts of fruit smoothies and hardboiled eggs, but also avoid smoking, liquor, and caffeine. This, of course, was Mormon doctrine as well, our own special Word of Wisdom, given by God through his prophets in the nineteenth century, so that we might run and not be weary and walk and not faint. I smiled because when she talked about keeping our bodies clean, or saving sex for marriage, or spending special time every Monday night with our families, I knew Marie was talking directly to me, to the sacred beliefs we shared in common. I smiled because Marie, Way Bandy, Yusuke Suga, Bob the cameraman, and all the other celebrity stylists and editors could even make our homely Mormon doctrines and customs so convincing and effortlessly gorgeous.

My very favorite advice in the whole book appeared on a page with a soft-focus photograph of Marie, wearing a tailored plaid blouse, lying on her belly in front of a row of blossoming tulips, chin tilted downward, caressing and speaking gently to a German shepherd pup. I could take stock of myself, she advised, my good points and my bad points. I could make a list, a bullet-point list, precisely numbered, of all the good. And although it might be difficult, I could also make a list, a bullet-point list, precisely numbered, of all the bad, whether it be shyness, or bossiness, or insecurity. With practice, I could improve. With practice, I could transform my minuses into plusses. "Just like dieting or studying or improving your voice, you have to practice to be perfect," Marie wrote, and who would know better? "Not only will it make you feel better about yourself, it will make others more receptive to you."

There was a song we learned to sing on Sundays in our Young Women's classes:

*I want to be a window to His love,*
*so when you look at me you will see Him.*
*I want to be so pure and clear*
*that you won't even know I'm here,*
*'cause His love will shine brightly through me.*

I too wanted to be pure and clear, an open door, a spotless window. I wanted the love of God to shine brightly through me like a perfect frame, no bitten nails, or blemishes, or extra pounds, flyaway hairs, or personal character minuses to bar the view of His eternal brightness. What, after all, was the point of the small but burdensome body I freighted about in these middling years, when already I knew, I knew, that beyond this life there was a place of total understanding, and already I hungered to evaporate into it.

Marie, I know that like me you were taught to "be ye therefore perfect," as Jesus said, but that being Mormons we were taught never to go in for the bamboozle of mysterious sacraments of grace embraced by the rest of apostate Christendom. No priests in dresses placing brittle emblems of salvation on our tongues; no sudden ecstasy of renovating seizure by the Holy Ghost. No, no, we Mormons were taught that our works must carry us there, that our works would make us perfect enough for God to finally recognize us as worthy of His love.

I would be lying, though, Marie, if I did not tell you that even at twelve years old I sensed beyond the polish of your celebrity prose the urgent subtext of your program for personal perfection. I saw it there on page ninety-three, in the self-abnegating caption under the picture of long-haired, chubby Marie making a plate full of ham and cheese sandwiches in the Osmond family kitchen: "This is *not* the way to diet!"

You and me, Marie, wrestling the dark energies of childhood depressions and nascent eating disorders. You and me, with visions of self-harm, dark impulses we could only describe as religious. These wars with our own bodies, how did we understand them but as a battle against the traitorous flesh that stood between us and our holiest inner selves, that stood between us and God?

What to do with our bodies? If they were not instruments of priesthood power, and not yet instruments of eternal procreation, what was our purpose? It was you, Marie, who gave me the doctrine of the wardrobe grid, the seven quick and healthy breakfast plans, three makeup personalities, the sanctifying discipline of daily reducing exercises, the promise that I could have as much diet gelatin, chicken bullion, or vinegar-dressed salad as I wanted and still keep my diet virtue. Impossible as all these regimens were for a girl like me without a team of celebrity stylists, or a car, or even a few dollars to spend on sable-hair brushes at the local drug store, Marie, your precisely numbered regimens gave me great comfort. Especially the idea that with a little *practice* I could change, I could convert those long columns of personal minuses into a perfect string of plusses.

For when I was lying there at twelve years old on the brown carpet in the early morning hours with *Marie*

*Osmond's Guide to Beauty, Health & Style* by my side, doing my calisthenics by the light of the clock radio, I felt that in time, with enough discipline, and a few implements from the local drugstore, I too might fade away into nothing at all.

I could dissolve under the heat of stage lights into a shimmer of perfection.

I could be so pure and clear, no one would know I was even here.

I too might disappear.

# 5

# mormons vs. born-agains

## dance-off, rose bowl, 1985

It was the summer of the great Mormon Dance Festival of 1985. I was just thirteen years old. But I knew that there was no place I'd rather be than among fifteen thousand strapping, sateen-clad young California Mormons moving in precisely choreographed patterns across the floor of the world-famous Rose Bowl. The sight of all of us youth of the latter days: God would be so stoked!

So I enlisted with all my thirteen-year-old girlfriends—Natasha, Shirley, Shayne, Charlotte—and we were assigned, as were all of the other thirteen-year-old girls in Southern California, to the all-girls' "Singin' in the Rain" number. Wednesday and Saturday afternoons, down at the church cultural hall, we learned to dance in time with Gene Kelly. Umbrellas—*left, then right, then left, then right*. It was no wonder that Mormon girls willing to participate in the great

Mormon Dance Festival of 1985 outnumbered willing Mormon boys. Oh no. Just one look down the pew each Sunday at the pock-faced dorks who were my Mormon male contemporaries and the perfectly groomed Mormon girls with their ribbons tied and their scriptures poised serenely on their laps and I knew that faithful girls would always outnumber faithful boys. Which is why, of course, polygamy was inevitable in the highest levels of heaven. Girls would certainly outnumber boys there, and everyone had to marry to get in, or else remain single, a ministering angel, in the third-highest level in heaven. An eternal A–.

At least we girls would always have each other, whether as ministering angels, or plural wives. That much we could count on. And on Saturdays my skinny redheaded best friend Natasha, Shayne, Charlotte, Shirley, and I learned how to move together as pieces of a soon-to-be cosmic whole. *Left, then right, left again, and right again*; chorus line, spinning wheel, square. Yes, we Mormons needed one another.

Especially because here in California, outside Idaho, Utah, and Arizona, we were so vastly outnumbered. Not as outnumbered, of course, as the kids who lived in improbable Mormon places like Florida, New York, Ohio, or Michigan, places our forethinking ancestors had abandoned generations ago for their westward trek. Why would you ever go back? We Mormons in California at least had the wisdom to realize the full arc of our people's trajectory, pushing past the western rim of the Great Basin, through the desert passes, and down to the incomparable beaches of Southern California.

But California also presented special challenges, for though we Mormons were few, we were many enough to get the attention of the local born-again Christians. Orange County in particular was home to tens of thousands of born-agains. On Sundays, they filled up great stuccoed stadium-style megachurches with one-word names: Melodyland. Calvary. Saddleback. No more *Methodist*, *Baptist*, *Presbyterian*—empty words rooted in archaic European schisms. For the orange-grove suburbs were full of people who had moved from somewhere else, ready to forget everything, even the names of their ancestral Christian denominations. Forget it all. That was the born-again way: just confess the name of Jesus, say *Jesus-I-take-you-into-my-heart* and poof! it could all be sun bleached away into a sanctified balm of year-round 70-degree weather and swaying palms.

Born-agains. There were so many of them. And I wouldn't care, except for the fact that their born-again pastors had declared battle against Mormons. Yes, at some point all of the megachurch pastors had gotten together and decided that Mormonism was a dangerous cult that needed confrontation, and the born-again kids, they took this quite seriously. One day in seventh grade I opened my locker door to find a typed-up screed taped inside. It accused me of believing in the wrong Jesus. Another day, in pre-algebra, an unsigned note came down the row of desks to me, bearing an ominous message warning me to get to the summer megarevival at Angel Stadium. Someone even scribbled little "John 3:16" warnings throughout my yearbook.

And if these daytime indignities were not enough, every night the air around me was saturated with invisible radio waves of anti-Mormonism, which spiraled out into the dark over the orange groves from a studio down the freeway in San Juan Capistrano. "This is Dr. Walter Martin, the Bible Answer Man, coming to you live from the Christian Research Institute in Southern California," the broadcasts began. Dr. Walter Martin was definitely at war: against us, Seventh-day Adventists, Hare Krishnas, and UFOs, and everything and everyone else he considered enemies of Jesus. He especially liked to make fun of the Mormon teaching that the Spirit speaks to us by a burning in our bosoms. "How do you know," he would intone, I imagined, leaning into the microphone, greasy comb-over, eyes closed, "that's not a bad bit of beef you've eaten?"

The smartest Mormon boy I knew, fifteen-year-old Garrett Jones, who wore big square glasses, would phone in to the station just to give Dr. Walter Martin a hard time. He'd dial up during the call-in segments and push back on Martin point for point, speaking in a deep, superrational, grown-up sounding voice. I did not have a deep, superrational voice, and I thought it very brave of Garrett to battle back against the Bible Answer Man. Even if he was hopelessly outnumbered as the only Mormon calling into the show. Even if all of us Mormons were hopelessly outnumbered.

Even if he was all alone.

One night my friend Jeannette (who was a born-again Christian) invited me to The Door, a youth gathering at the giant six-thousand-member Calvary Church. I walked in and scanned the room to see if I could recognize any other Mormon kids—but I was all alone. Hundreds of born-again kids sat at long tables in the dark auditorium, passing free pizza on thin paper plates down the rows. Rock music boomed from the loudspeakers: some kind of Christian Bachman-Turner Overdrive. The *real* BTO was Mormon, *thank you very much.*

Jeannette and I found seats. Out of the darkness, plates of pizza arrived, and a stand-up comic materialized on a makeshift stage in the gym. He had dark hair, a puffy face, a thick middle; he wore rumpled, baggy pants, a Windbreaker, and white basketball high-tops. The comic told ten minutes of car crash jokes, pacing and waving his arms in the air. And then, throwing a dramatic switch, he arrived at his *very important message*:

"Now, kids," he said, stepping to the front of the makeshift stage, bringing his microphone in close to his chest. The rock music stopped. The comic drew a serious expression.

"I want you to know . . ." (dramatic pause) "that the Mormon Church is a cult."

I swallowed hard. Anger burned between my temples. Again, I scanned the room to see if I could find other Mormons.

"The Mormons say that the Bible is the word of God insofar as it is translated correctly."

The comic paused for dramatic effect, scanning the crowds under a scrim of feathered dark bangs, looking for approval.

"Well, let me tell you, I have seen the original manuscripts from which the Bible is translated, and it *is* translated correctly."

With hard eyes, I scrutinized the anti-Mormon comic: his baggy pants, Windbreaker, and high-tops. If you're such a genius of original scriptural translation, I thought, if you have *seen* the *original Bible* (one set of manuscripts? where?) and can verify its translated accuracy (against which of the fifty-five watered down vernacular translations you people use, no match for our mighty King James version), what are you doing performing anti-Mormon stand-up comedy routines for high school crowds in Orange County, California, on Friday night?

"So, whatever you do, remember that you must be born again, you must take Jesus into your heart to be saved. Thank you." He threw a fist into the air, the lights clamped off, the fake Bachman-Turner Overdrive came back on, and all the born-again kids went wild.

In the dark, I looked at my friend Jeannette, redheaded, pink eyed, sniffing nervously like the rabbits she raised and showed at 4-H.

Did she bring me here knowing this would be the evening's entertainment? Did she bring me here to save me, or shame me? Did she imagine this spiritual battle against Mormonism was for my benefit?

I hung on to my seat and waited for the pizza to run out.

But of all the indignities one could suffer as a thirteen-year-old Mormon girl, the worst to me by far was the fact that a movie called *The God Makers* was making the rounds of all the local churches. *The God Makers* was the work of a disgruntled former Mormon, who depicted our heaven as a realm of faraway planets with funny names, where double-talking men had celestial sex with polygamous goddess wives who wanted to be eternally pregnant. *The God Makers* even made a mockery of what happened in our Mormon temples, lampooning the choreography of promises our parents, grandparents, and great-grandparents rehearsed behind closed doors. They made fun of our parents' underwear too.

For months I watched church marquees across town feature the words THE GODMAKERS or the phrase MORMONS: CHRISTIAN OR CULT? I desperately hoped the movie would not make it to Trinity Presbyterian, the church attended by hundreds of kids at my junior high school. Every week, on my way to piano lessons at Sister Collier's house, we passed by Trinity. Every time I'd brace myself to see the marquee, just as we rounded the corner on 17th Street.

And then it happened. My mother put her hand on my knee as we made the turn. There they were, those words—MORMONS: CHRISTIAN OR CULT?—on the Trinity marquee. Anger burned between my temples again, and tears stung my eyes. "I heard they held up garments in church last Sunday too," my mother told me, pityingly, reassuringly.

Why us? What did they want from us, those born-agains? And what was it, exactly, besides the talk about us being a cult, and the underwear, and the temples, and the planets, and the fact that they said Joseph Smith was in league with the devil, and we worshipped the wrong Jesus, what was it they needed to battle?

"We're growing," my mother explained in a calm, super-rational voice. "We're taking converts. They're threatened."

Threatening? Us? Mormons? With our family vans, ten children apiece, our tins of vacuum-packed wheat stored up against the apocalypse, our homely calico pioneer bonnets, our heavy books of genealogy, our home-baked bread, our Utah, our world-famous choir, Gordon Jump, and Bachman-Turner Overdrive? Us?

Early on dance festival morning, thousands of us Mormon youth across the Southland packed our sateen spangled costumes in our duffle bags, climbed into our family vans, and trekked up the freeway to the world-famous Rose Bowl. Mormon kids from farther-flung California places arrived in yellow school buses. Standing in the dusty parking lot, I watched bus after bus pour in, the names of their home cities posted in the windows: San Luis Obispo, Blythe, Bakersfield, Ventura, Poway, Poway, Poway.

What heaven Poway must have been, I thought, with so many Mormons there.

Natasha, Charlotte, Shayne, Shirley, and I cruised around and around the Rose Bowl parking lot in our modest knee-length shorts and Brigham Young University T-shirts, giddy at the sight of so many Mormons in one place, riding what felt like a red-punch-and-sugar-cookie high. In the morning we rehearsed our moves in dusty quadrants of the Rose Bowl grounds—umbrellas swinging left, then right, then left, then right. After lunch, we moved out onto the legendary Rose Bowl turf to experience the wonder of thousands of "Singin' in the Rain" dancers moving in precisely choreographed circles, zigzags, and lines.

After our final run-through, in the late afternoon heat, the dance festival organizers herded us all into the Rose Bowl stands and set up microphones on the grassy gridiron, so that Mormon youth from all over Southern California could bear testimony of the truthfulness of the gospel, expressing to one another our love for the Mormon Church and the teachings that kept us safe and together in these latter days. A young man in his twenties, one of the older dance festival participants, a returned missionary fresh back from Chile wearing modest knee-length shorts, stood at the microphone and proposed marriage to his girlfriend in the stands.

As the sun set over the smoggy San Gabriel Mountains, our master of ceremonies materialized: beloved Mormon television star Gordon Jump of *WKRP in Cincinnati*.

Gordon Jump rode out onto the field in a little jeep, greeted us, and then gave the word. We all deployed to carefully segregated bays of the great concrete Rose Bowl to change into our spangly, sateen dance festival costumes sewn up in some faraway subtropical factory town.

That's when the first of the fifty thousand Mormon spectators began to arrive at the Rose Bowl parking lot. Wood-sided station wagons loaded with kids and coolers of cold cuts, Jell-O salads, and supermarket-brand grape soda started to clog up the freeway off-ramps to Pasadena. When one station wagon broke down, exhaust swirling around its tires, almost immediately another station wagon or, better yet, a family van would pull up alongside. "Can we help you? Hop on in!"

Lost a wallet at the Rose Bowl? It would come back in the mail, intact, postage paid.

Small children who wandered away from parents into the festival crowds? Safe as lambs.

Will you go a mile with me? Heck, I'll go an extra mile.

That's the sort of thing that happened when sixty-five thousand Mormons got together.

Of course, the born-agains couldn't resist, and they sent an especially brave delegation to do battle against all sixty-five thousand of us. About a dozen anti-Mormon picketers stood at the Rose Bowl gates, looping their signs in the air. In those days there were always a few picketers outside our churches or temples, telling us that we didn't believe in the right Jesus. But with sixty-five thousand Mormons on the Rose Bowl grounds, fifteen thousand of them young people trained as precision dancers, the ragged little deployment of born-agains didn't have a chance. A group of Mormon kids encircled them and began to sing our beloved hymn, "I am a Child of God," the very sound of which so confounded our tormentors that they withered and vaporized into thin air.

At least that's what my best friend Natasha told me she heard from a girl in the cha-cha number.

There were other Mormon and Mormon-friendly celebrities on hand for the festivities: football great Merlin Olsen (now of *Little House on the Prairie*), star quarterback Steve Young (great-great-great grandson of Brigham), Mrs. America 1984 Debbie Wolf, America's Sweethearts the Lennon Sisters of Lawrence Welk fame, and at least three Osmond brothers.

First number up: one thousand couples in hot pink and orange Carmen Miranda dresses and matching suits dancing the cha-cha.

Next came a thousand couples in silver-and-gold sateen to do the Charleston and the jitterbug to the sounds of the Glenn Miller Orchestra.

A thousand more couples in neon yellow-and-green sateen with suspenders bopped to Bill Haley's "Rock Around the Clock" and the Beach Boys' "Surfin' USA."

Then one thousand couples in orange and royal blue danced a Virginia reel–style tribute to our Mormon pioneer ancestors, who, history tells us, danced their troubles away round the campfires during their trek across the plains.

My number was next: "Singin' in the Rain," a thousand thirteen-year-old girls like me and Natasha in rainbow-colored (and precision sequenced) sateen dresses with clear plastic raincoats swinging white umbrellas—*right, then left, then right, then left*.

After we cleared the field, a thousand couples in black tuxedos and white bridelike dresses waltzed in to take our place.

Then came a thousand male and female cheerleaders in striped red-and-white jumpsuits, with pom-poms, bouncing about to the fight songs for our Brigham Young University and the University of Utah.

A thousand couples in dirndls and lederhosen, looking like Disneyland employees, did the polka in tribute to immigrant America, under the watchful gaze of a miniature Statue of Liberty stationed on the sidelines.

Finally came the four Lennon Sisters, all wearing green sequined dresses, crammed into a little red sleigh, on a white sheet, in the middle of the Rose Bowl field, to sing a Christmas song surrounded by a thousand swaying Mormon youth in white tuxedos and red velvet dresses.

"Isn't it wonderful that as Americans we have the freedom to celebrate religion as we choose?" said one of the Lennon Sisters, as the rest chimed in, "Oh, yes."

"And isn't it wonderful that as *Christians*, Mormons celebrate the birth of our *Savior* Jesus Christ?"

*Oh, yes: Take that, born-agains!*

We were just thirteen, my skinny friend Natasha and I, but we understood the power of the moment when we crowded with fifteen thousand Mormon youth in the dark tunnels of the Rose Bowl, ready to burst onto the fields for the dance festival grand finale. As went the words to our beloved Mormon hymn:

*Shall the youth of Zion falter*
*In defending truth and right*
*While the enemy assaileth,*
*Shall we shrink or shun the fight? No!*

*True to the faith that our parents have cherished*
*True to the truth for which martyrs have perished*
*To God's command*
*Soul, heart, and hand*
*Faithful and true we will ever stand*

We were proud Mormon youth of Zion in the last days, none of us shrinking or shunning the fight, a legion of amateur Osmonds primed to appear in paradisiacal glory, and so we would ever stand.

And as the sun set deep behind the smoggy San Gabriel Mountains, as I felt the bodies crowding in the tunnel around me, I thought to myself:

I'd like to see the born-agains pull this off.

I'd like to see them muster this degree of regimentation.

They couldn't even coordinate the made-up names of their franchise churches: Calvary, Melodyland, the Rock.

What did these people know about discipline and commitment?

Did they go to church at six a.m. every morning before school, as Mormon kids did?

Had they disciplined their minds for the possibility that God would ask them to take a second wife into the family in order to get to heaven? No, all they had to do to get to heaven was read a prayer from a mass-produced Tony Alamo pamphlet about accepting Jesus into your heart. All they had to do was say, "I accept you, Jesus, as my savior," just like that. Poof.

Had they drilled the stories and teachings of four—that's right, *four*—books of scripture into their heads? No, just one, just the Bible.

Had they carefully sealed up tins of rice and textured vegetable protein against the great and final days? Were they ready to live through the end-times? No, while they dreamed of being transported up into the clouds like *Star Trek*, we were ready to live out the nuclear winter that would follow the second coming of Christ, to rebuild a kingdom from the charred timbers of leveled forests.

Those born-agains could never do what we did. Cross the plains. Track down and baptize our dead ancestors by the millions. Fan out all over the globe two by two, knocking on doors. Precision coordinate fifteen thousand teenage dancers.

What it all came down to was this: those born-agains were soft.

I felt clean Mormon bodies encased in flammable sateen, bodies raised on casseroles, bodies free of caffeine and other worldly abuses packed in the Rose Bowl tunnel around me.

Maybe *he* is here tonight, I thought to myself.

Maybe *he* is here, wearing a neon green-and-yellow sateen outfit.

Maybe *he* came on one of those buses from Poway, my someday love, my future Mormon husband.

When the signal came, fifteen thousand of us rushed through the tunnels and down into the stadium. We roared fifteen thousand strong, and fifty thousand Mormon spectators roared back. Red pom-pom, now blue pom-pom, a sea of patriotic precision: "From everywhere around the world, they come to America . . ."

Natasha and I shook our blue pom-poms in the warm July night, feeling the triumphant legacy of the great concrete Rose Bowl, feeling too the strength of our Mormon nation, gathered in from every corner of the world. We waved our pom-poms for Utah, for pioneer grandmothers, for wheat sealed in tins against the apocalypse, for our sacred temples on killer real estate all across California, and broken-down station wagons rescued tonight in the swirling smog of the Pasadena freeways. We waved our pom-poms for Gordon Jump, calico bonnets, and Bachman-Tuner Overdrive, and against *The God Makers*, and the anti-Mormon stand-up comic in his rumpled khakis, and Jeannette, and all the born-again Christians who said they wanted to be my friends, and their pastors too. I waved my pom-pom because I was not afraid of polygamy, sacred underwear, or the idea of eternal godhood, and neither were the fifteen thousand youth in flammable sateen outfits moving in majestic precision on the field around me. I was not the only one who believed in worlds as numberless as the stars in the sky. Why not? *Why the heck not?*

"Today!" The voice of Neil Diamond burst overhead like fireworks.

"Today!" A stadium of Mormons came to their feet.

Today! I felt a burning in my heart. Somewhere under these lights, on the Rose Bowl field, *he* was here: my future husband, *the One*, he who would understand my Mormon world without my defending or explaining.

Tonight, true to the faith, he was here just like me, dancing in flammable sateen to the sounds of Neil Diamond and Kool and the Gang.

# 6

# sister williams's tampons

Sister Tucker stood almost six feet tall, with short white hair and sharp eyes in a pretty face. Sister Larsen was five foot two, quick tongued, smart-alecky, and redheaded. Sister Williams had wide hips and soft hands; her short hair was feathered like the wings of doves and her accent was Utah gentle. Sister Barnes had thick ankles and thick glasses, her face lined with deep intelligence. Between them, they had born and raised twenty-four children. None of them foolish, weak, or neurotic; all of them uncomplaining bearers of sixty-pound packs—these were our Girls Camp leaders.

And it was their job to take us, a dozen fifteen-year-old Mormon girls, up into the High Sierras, to teach us the basics of wilderness survival through the Mormon Campcrafter program. For months we had met down at the church on Tuesday afternoons, mastering each of the Campcrafter skills, learning to tie boat-line knots, build fires, lash tables, and administer first aid. We had selected our external frame backpacks and backpacker tents from the congregation's vast inventory, stored in Sister Tucker's garage. Only thirty pounds, Sister Williams had instructed. We'd be hiking a talus-littered trail up to ten thousand feet, after all, and then spend three days creekside among the lodgepole pines. This was not the time to pack a mini Pac-Man game (Natasha!) or cans of SpaghettiOs (Shirley!).

The first morning of Girls Camp, we loaded into Sister Williams's blue Econoline family van. It seems like every other family in the ward had a blue Econoline family van, with bench seats—not captain's chairs—and hose-down floor mats. It was the perfect vehicle in which to haul about one's natural-born nine children, as Sister Williams did, or a pack of fifteen-year-old girls to camp in the High Sierras. The van left our orange grove suburb, wound through the Los Angeles freeway system, and started the long ride up California Highway 395. In the Owens Valley, we passed old mining towns, crystalline lake beds, and prison camps. A left turn took us away from the arid valley floor and into the glacier-carved Eastern Sierras.

The van doors popped open. Out we stepped—Sister Williams, Sister Larsen, Natasha, Shayne, Charlotte, Shirley, Kristi, and me from the one van; Sister Tucker, Sister Barnes, Jennifer, Jennifer, Juli, Missy, Tammi, and Joy from the other. We hoisted our packs onto our backs, cinching the belts until the edges lodged on the tops of our fifteen-year-old hip bones, and set out on the four-mile trail to Tom's Place. The air was already thin at seven thousand feet, the trail steep and rocky. Within minutes of leaving the parking lot, I was sucking air between my teeth, trying to will away an attack of my childhood asthma: *gasp, caw, gasp, caw.* Natasha's shoes came untied, and she dragged the laces along through the rocks. At a switchback water break, Shirley wobbled over, her ankles unsteady, and leaned down to help. A can of SpaghettiOs rolled out of her pack and off the side of the trail into the manzanita.

Sister Williams and Sister Barnes brought up the rear of the group; Sister Larsen and Sister Tucker led. "One foot in front of the other," she called back to us stragglers. One foot in front of the other was what I did.

Maybe it was just my oxygen-deprived brain—*gasp, caw, gasp, caw*—but it struck me that Sister Tucker's words held the key to, well, *everything.* Yes, with every foot Natasha, Shirley, and I ascended, the world around us assumed a kind of luminescent meaningfulness. Everything was haloed with spiritual significance—from the jagged granite peaks ahead of us, to the glacier-carved valleys, to the yarrow and mule ears at the creeksides. *Gasp, caw, gasp, caw.* I fixed my eyes at the head of the line of backpackers, on the back of Sister Tucker's head, her brilliant white hair. One foot in front of the other. It was difficult, sometimes, being a fifteen-year-old Mormon girl, with scrawny lungs, a bad perm, and wobbly ankles. But this was the very point of it, the very point of *everything*: our spirits had been sent to earth to persist against the weak and messy medium of our bodies, one foot in front of the other, until we reached higher places. That was the lesson we came to Girls Camp to learn.

A white tennis shoe dropped from Shirley's backpack. I stopped and gulped down air. Sister Williams placed her feet in a wide stance, eased down to reach the shoe, while balancing her pack on her capable hips, and tied the shoe to the back of Shirley's external frame pack.

*Gasp, caw, gasp, caw*—we resumed our trudge up the mountain.

When night fell in the Eastern Sierras, we had reached our camp, set up our backpacker tents, unrolled our sleeping bags, gathered up wood, and set foil dinners to cook on campfire coals.

We gathered around the fire and lodged our backs against fallen pines. Sister Tucker, Sister Williams, Sister Larsen, and Sister Barnes took their place among us. We ate warmed peas and carrots and potatoes from our foil packets, and washed them down with canteens of water pumped from the glacier-fed creek.

So many questions we had about the mysteries of our impending Mormon womanhood. So many things we could not ask on a regular Sunday at home, locked inside the cold cinder-block-walled church, tied up in Sunday dresses. Where better to talk about these matters than up here at eleven thousand feet, under the guidance of four unflinching Mormon women?

The fire crackled. Natasha shifted against the log. I swallowed hard and looked at Sister Tucker.

"Will there be polygamy in heaven?" I asked.

Everyone knew that the Church had officially stopped polygamy in 1890. But Mormon doctrine still taught that one had to be married to enter the highest realms of heaven. And polygamy was still in our scriptures. And sometimes, even in these latter days, men who had lost a first wife were sealed for time and all eternity to a second wife as well. There was plenty of reason to believe there would be polygamy in heaven, and the topic always hovered at the back of female conversation.

"Your father and I have discussed it," my mother would tell me from time to time, a white-hot metal edge to her voice, her words terse and final. "He will not do that to me."

Sometimes, at church parties, with all the women in the kitchen heating so many spiral-sliced hams and trays of homemade wheat rolls, an older woman would joke, "Now, girls, can't you see the sense in polygamy?" which would make the younger women laugh, or lower their heads, or grumble wearily.

How did Sister Larsen, Sister Williams, Sister Tucker, and Sister Barnes reckon it?

There was a pause. Sister Tucker looked at Sister Barnes, the firelight reflecting in her thick glasses.

"You know," Sister Barnes offered, "some difficult things, we just put them on a shelf until we can take them up with God directly." In her face I could see a wisdom without edge, a patient deferral of certainty, the very crux of faith: *one foot in front of the other.*

If God was indeed merciful, I thought, I would not spend the eternities living in second-fiddle misery. But if it were indeed the rule that you had to be married to go to heaven, and if there were (as all appearances suggested) so many more righteous women than men in the world, would I refuse to share my husband, even if it meant keeping a sister out of heaven?

The stars turned like screws in the black skies.

No, I decided, I was not so enthralled by the earthly ideal of single marriage that I would lock another woman out of the eternities.

And maybe it was not as we imagined, this polygamy. Perhaps it was a gesture toward a vaster spiritual truth, the outlines of which my oxygen-deprived brain could begin to perceive as I stared into the fire. Perhaps none of us entered the eternities alone, but with our souls all hooked together, multiply, through and across the generations, a kind of eternal belonging the grammar of companionate marriage could never capture. Up in the Sierras, my mind could begin to encompass such an idea.

My thinking was interrupted when Natasha blurted out question number two.

"Do you have to wear your garments on your wedding night?" she asked.

Shirley, Joy, and Shayne coughed and giggled. But we had a right to know. Did we really have to wear the knee-length, shoulder-capping Mormon undergarments our parents and grandparents wore, embroidered with simple markings to remind us of our promises to live faithful Mormon lives? These and not the curious red-and-black satin contraptions we saw in shop windows at the mall, the sex costumes the world prescribed?

Sister Tucker looked at Sister Williams. Sister Williams looked at Sister Larsen and smiled. Sister Larsen leaned over to Sister Tucker and whispered something behind cupped hands. Sister Tucker laughed and nodded.

"Yes, of course," Sister Larsen said. "You'll wear your garments on your wedding night so that you can have the fun of your husband taking them off!"

These questions of sex were not just curiosity seeking. Our whole Mormon world was organized into domains of the male and female.

We saw that women did not:

hold the priesthood
prepare, bless, or pass the bread and water sacrament
preside in meetings where men were present
receive tithing
make or keep records of tithing or other monetary offerings
make or keep membership records
give the closing prayer in church meetings
wear pants at church
perform baptisms, confirmations, ordinations, and marriages
conduct funerals
hear confessions
anoint or heal the sick
provide spiritual counsel to men
receive revelations for anyone besides themselves and their children

Conversely, we saw that men did not:

supervise the nursery for children under the age of three
teach the young women
preside over the women's Relief Society

A few of us remembered or had read in slim volumes of Mormon women's history that women had once:

healed the sick by the laying on of hands
blessed and anointed one another's bodies for
    childbirth
prophesied
spoken in tongues

But these powers had generally fallen out of practice in the early twentieth century.

The actual work of being in charge, receiving revelations, and presiding over home and church belonged exclusively to men. We had motherhood; men had priesthood. Their priesthood authority, we were taught, made up for their inability to bear children. For if God did not give them a big priesthood consolation prize, the story went, what other purpose would they serve in this life? What powers to compare to the lauded marvels of motherhood?

But those marvels seemed light years away to me. I had gotten my first period only a few months before Girls Camp, and no special ceremony marked the onset of my procreative powers. Numb to the silent inner workings of my own pelvis, I had discovered alone the black stain in my underpants in the stall of the yellow-tiled school bathroom. I told no one until I got home from school. Standing in the driveway, my mother and grandmother turned their faces away from me and to each other and laughed. "It's the curse, the curse, *the curse of the world*—that's what my mother always said," explained my Utah-born grandmother, her voice for once strangely devoid of tenderness.

Alone into the bathroom I went with a box of tampons; my fingers trembling and slippery, I swallowed hard and put the tampon inside myself.

That Sunday I sat in our regular pew, silent and bleeding, my breasts and belly a riot of puffiness and pain, while the boys my age stood before the congregation in clean white shirts to prepare and pass the white bread and tap water that was our sacrament.

On Sundays no one really talked about actual feats of women's power, the physical heroics of making and losing and bearing and nursing the many Mormon babies who filled our pews and punctuated our meetings with their cries. Nowhere in the scriptures was there any special mapping of the spiritual domain of women. But around the fire at Girls Camp, we could prod Sister Larsen, Sister Williams, Sister Barnes, and Sister Tucker into recounting, as if from a secret canon, brave epics of women's labors and deliveries.

"Tell it again," we begged Sister Barnes. "Tell us the one about Mexico."

Sister Barnes was the mother of nine children. She belonged to a vast sixth-generation Mormon family, with its roots among the earliest followers of Joseph Smith, and branches that extended out into the Mormon colonies of northern Mexico, where many of the most faithful had fled after the Mormon Church's official abolition of polygamy, to continue the practice beyond the reach of United States law.

Her eldest daughter Laurie married at nineteen and with her Idaho farm-boy husband settled into a little basement apartment south of the Brigham Young University campus. They were poor as church mice, and very soon they were pregnant.

Sister Barnes lived in the nearby town of Orem. One day she was standing in the kitchen ironing her way through a giant pile of men's white Sunday shirts when Laurie called to say she was in labor. "Let me finish this basket of shirts," Sister Barnes told her daughter, "and then I'll be right over."

Sister Barnes finished the shirts, turned on the slow-cooker to start dinner, wrote her husband a little note, grabbed her purse, and hopped into her blue Econoline family van. There was no money to have the baby in the hospital. "Let's go see Uncle Vern," she told Laurie. "He can deliver it for you."

Sister Barnes helped Laurie up the steps of the basement apartment and into the back of the van, and the two set out down Highway 89 to see Uncle Vern, who had in fact delivered many, many babies during his decades in the little Mormon settlement of Colonia Juárez, Chihuahua, Mexico.

It was early afternoon. If they made good time, they could get to Mexico in about fifteen hours. Plenty of time for a first labor, Sister Barnes knew, having had nine children of her own.

Down Highway 89 through the little Mormon towns of Richfield, Panguitch, and Kanab flew the blue Econoline van. Laurie started to wince. "You'll be fine," Sister Barnes hollered back over her shoulder, elbows wide across the steering wheel as she piloted the red rock canyons of southern Utah and northern Arizona.

Winces became grimaces. At a gas station in Cameron, on the Navajo reservation, Sister Barnes hustled in to pick up a six-pack of Sprite. Laurie was now lying on the floor, twisting and turning, gamely trying to find a comfortable place between the bench seats. Sister Barnes opened the van doors, handed Laurie a Sprite, said, "Drink this," then shut the van doors and got back in the driver's seat.

As darkness fell, the van bumped on down through the Sonoran Desert, down through the White Mountains, down into and through small Mormon mining towns of southern Arizona. Sister Barnes could hear Laurie's pains steadying, cries sharper, intervals shorter. Her foot pressed against the gas.

"Laurie, you've got to sit up and be quiet now," Sister Barnes commanded when they pulled up to the border crossing at Agua Prieta, a single spot of light on the vast desert frontier. Sister Barnes smiled brightly, using the Spanish she remembered from her summer visits to cousins in the colonies. The border guards shined their flashlights into the windows of the van. Somehow Laurie, deep into her transition phase, pants wet with amniotic fluid, managed to hoist herself upright, clutch her empty Sprite, and grit her teeth in the shape of a smile. The guards waved and the blue Econoline lurched on, kicking up dust in the darkness.

When they pulled into Colonia Juárez, it was early morning. Uncle Vern was out hunting turkeys, and a cousin was dispatched to find him. The last thing Laurie remembered was being led into the clinic, then seeing a white-masked nurse douse a tray of medical instruments in rubbing alcohol and toss a match on top of them. Flames leaped three feet into the air. Next thing she knew, Laurie came to with a black-haired baby girl at her side, and Uncle Vern smiling down at her.

After three days and two nights at eleven thousand feet, we packed our tents, hoisted our packs back onto our hips, and descended the High Sierras, picking our way back across the talus slopes and down through the Jeffrey pines. Natasha, Shayne, Shirley, Joy, Charlotte, and our ensemble of Girls Camp leaders—we were all as dirty as Boy Scouts, our noses filled with campfire soot, our legs insect bitten and unshaven.

Back into the Econoline van we packed, and with Sister Williams at the wheel, returned to Highway 395, passing

Bishop, Lone Pine, Independence, the small towns and dry lake beds of the Owens Valley.

It was dark and late by the time we reached California City, the one-stop-sign town that marked the edge of the high desert. All the other girls had conked out in the first three rows of the van, their scraggly heads pushed up against the windows, their mouths wide open. But on the back bench seat my friend Natasha and I were wide awake, giddy, and filthy. Holding warm cups of root beer between our knees, we rummaged around the cargo-strewn floor of the van for something to entertain us.

Then we found it: a small blue Coleman cooler, the name WILLIAMS written in magic marker across the lid, and inside a cache of *the largest tampons we had ever seen*. Fatter than fingers! Fatter than shotgun shells! As we beheld their size and sheer number, Natasha and I dissolved in the backseat, our mouths frozen round.

I looked up in horror and awe at Sister Williams, the mother of nine blond Williams children, her face periodically illuminated by passing headlights in the rearview mirror. There she was, chatting happily with redheaded Sister Larsen in the passenger seat beside her, her elbows wide across the steering wheel, hips spilling over the driver's seat edge.

I tried not to derive from the size and number of these tampons information about the condition of Sister Williams's insides. I tried not to think about nine big-boned Williams children making their way down into the world. But there it was, in our laps, the evidence. *Giant tampons.* They looked nothing like the slender pink pearlescent tube I had learned to hold with slippery fingers just a few months before.

Did she get these on special order?

Natasha pulled a tampon from the cooler, stripped away its paper wrapper, pushed the cardboard plunger, and launched the jumbo wad of cotton into the warm cup of root beer between her knees. Silent laughter seized us as the cotton absorbed and expanded, filling the cup to its edges.

My mind rushed through the roof of the van out into the stars, and I saw the roles of men and women telescope outward to infinity: in the world of Mormonism, priesthood belonged to men, and motherhood to women, and these were not just temporary roles for this lifetime, but a pattern of what would be in the eternities. And we had been taught that only married couples could enter the highest realms of heaven, where they themselves attained the godly powers to frame worlds and populate them with spirit children. And we knew that our God, the Mormon God, was a set of Heavenly Parents—a Father, and a Mother, if not Mothers. Did this then suggest, by simple reasoning, that it would take a lot of spiritual procreating to generate the billions of souls who came to earth? And was I then to understand that if I worked hard enough to get to heaven, eternal pregnancy in the company of plural pregnant wives might very well be my reward?

Surely I had heard as much implied, in the murmuring tones of kitchen chatter at the ward dinner, in the panicked edge to my mother's voice.

My mind rushed back into my body in the backseat of the van, where Natasha and I were still peering, transfixed, into the cup, at Sister Williams's giant tampon and all that it inferred. Nine pregnancies. Nine children. Eternal pregnancy. Millions of spirit children. Children numbered like the grains of sand in the California desert, or like the stars in the desert skies.

I tried to put the whole matter on the shelf like Sister Barnes suggested; I tried to follow Sister Tucker's advice and put one foot in front of the other.

But I could not.

Instead, frozen with horror, I leaned into my best friend Natasha. The van bumped and jostled through the desert dark, kicking up dust and scattering jackrabbits into the brush. Who knows what Natasha was thinking, but I took comfort in the sound of her laughter as I tried to get used to the feeling of being in the backseat, never driving, always driven, headed for destinations not of my choosing and vast beyond my control.

# 7

# object lessons

When I was sixteen years old, LeVar Royal, the fifty-five-year-old "godfather of pool plastering," asked me to visit his office at the church.

LeVar (a Mormon name, to be sure) had salt-and-pepper hair and a beaklike nose. He spoke with a southern Idaho farm-boy accent, vast and flat as the plains he came from. Sometime in the 1950s, LeVar escaped that endless dirt horizon, married a pretty redhead, and came down the I-15 to California, where he won himself the title "godfather of pool plastering" by revolutionizing the industry with his trademark plastic trowel and cleats.

They say he plastered more than a quarter of a million pools in our orange grove suburbs. Trackless, like a spider, he glided all day across the bottom of empty swimming pools, trowel in hand, skin bronzing in the California sun.

At church, LeVar Royal held the office of stake president, which meant he oversaw the spiritual lives of two or three thousand Mormons, including me. He'd sidle up to you, slide an arm around your waist, give you a little wink and squeeze. He was Idaho smooth, smooth like volcanic loam running through the fingers.

His was no easy job, for sure, making sure that all the Mormons in our town were getting along, keeping the commandments, loving one another, and fulfilling the hundreds of volunteer offices it took to keep our clergy-free congregations running. His office was the place the most serious matters got ironed out—including the matter of our teenage virtue. All of the girls in the Stake were expected to see President Royal once, in their sixteenth year. When my turn came, I found myself not at all soothed by a friendly wink and a quick squeeze, but rather cringing in my own skin.

President Royal wore a dark business suit and sat in a high-back swivel chair behind the grand Formica-top desk ordered straight from Salt Lake City. I sat stiffly in my Sunday dress.

"Well," he began, leaning back to get a better look at me. The words burbled out, rising and falling, in that singsong Idaho way.

"You've come to that special time in your life when you are becoming a young lady."

My mind zoomed around the room, looking for a high window, a way out.

"And I know of the challenges you will face, and of the

tremendous blessings that lie in store. I have daughters, and I know the pains they bear. I have held their heads at those difficult times of the month."

I cringed. I imagined his daughters, basketball players, passed out on the sidelines, in the wooden bleachers, their sweaty heads in their father's hands.

"But as you come into your maturity, you should know most of all that your Heavenly Father expects that you will keep your purity and virtue about you. And *I* expect you to keep your virtue about you, until the day you are married in a temple of the Lord."

It was clear LeVar Royal had done this dozens of times, with dozens of other sixteen-year-old girls, each of whom had sat alone in this standard-issue Salt Lake City chair.

"Now, I want you to remember this talk we have had."

Smooth in his routine, President Royal opened the right-hand desk drawer. He withdrew a sky-blue velveteen jewelry box and slid it across the desktop to me.

"Go ahead and open it," he said.

The tight gold hinges on the box squeaked, then popped open. Inside, a faux-gold chain strung with a single pearl rested on a paper card.

I could feel the godfather of pool plastering search my face for a reaction. I kept my head down and pretended to admire the soft yellow chain.

"Now, if you are to lose your virtue before you marry, I want you to remember, you owe me a pearl necklace."

Perfectly composed, I shook LeVar Royal's hand and left his office. I have no idea what happened to the necklace—did I shove it in the back of a dresser drawer? did I throw it in the bushes?—other than to say that I know I never wore it.

So important it was to keep our virtue about us that our church leaders reserved entire weeknight meetings to offer us strict how-to instructions. On those Standards Nights, we all wore our Sunday dresses, and our Young Women's leaders draped the little tables in the church classrooms with lace tablecloths, dimmed the lights, and placed vases of white long-stemmed roses before us.

I would rather have been out in the church gym, dangling my legs and crossed ankles over the edge of the stage, gossiping and watching the sweaty boys run around bouncing basketballs.

I bet my teacher Sister Duncan would rather have been somewhere else too, maybe home baking bread for her husband, Boyd, a soft-spoken man who had lost one of his fingers in the war. But just as my father and mother did, so too Sister Duncan felt keenly the currents of worldly peril rushing around us on all sides. We were *her* girls. It was her job to keep us safe from the disastrous mess the MTV world made of men and women, safe until we could find someone like Brother Duncan to take us to the temple and promise to work hard and love us forever and ever. No, it was not an easy job talking to a room of sixteen-year-old girls about so sensitive a subject, but Sister Duncan set herself to it, a bird-voiced soldier.

So there I sat, along with Shayne, Juli, Jennifer, and Natasha, all of us in our Sunday dresses on a Wednesday evening, shifting on our metal folding chairs, the hollow sound of bouncing basketballs echoing in the halls.

Sister Duncan took one white rose from the vase and handed it to Shayne.

"I want each of you to take a turn with this rose," Sister Duncan told us. "Go ahead, smell its fragrance, feel the soft petals. Each of you, have a turn."

We did as we were told, one after another, pressing our noses into the velvety lobes and fingering the outer petals.

By the time the rose made it back to Sister Duncan, it was a different creature: its tight inner bud pried open, petals missing, others crimped and browning.

"Now, girls, who would want to take this rose home," she said, holding up the damaged flower, then drawing an untouched rose from the vase, "when they could have one as pure and delicate as this?"

Standards Nights were all about object lessons.

Some years, it was not roses but cupcakes, or doughnuts, passed from girl to girl around the semicircle of folding chairs, losing glaze or frosting, fingers getting sticky, and the inevitable question: "Who would like to eat this damaged doughnut? And who would rather have one of these untouched doughnuts here in this pink box?"

Natasha told me that once, in her old ward, the bishop stood before the girls pounding a series of nails into a board, then removing them one by one with the back end of his hammer.

"You see," he would say, holding the board up before them, "even when the nail is removed, the hole is still there, and there's nothing we can do to make it right again."

At Standards Night, they always taught the rules about things that are done with the body that must be confessed.

Kissing: okay.

French kissing: maybe okay, maybe not—be careful.

Light petting (breasts involved): must confess to bishop.

Heavy petting (below the waist involved): must confess to bishop.

Oral sex (unthinkable): must confess to bishop, possibly serious.

Fornication: must confess to bishop, definitely serious, may be required to confess before a court of church leaders, may be disfellowshipped.

I never had anything to confess until the summer after my freshman year in college. I had just promised myself to a blond boy from Orem, Utah. His name was John Swenson.

All spring, while the cherry trees blossomed on the hills, John Swenson stood under my second-floor dorm-room window making plaintive noises. One Sunday after dinner at his family home in Orem, I saw for the first time the miracle of the Utah irrigation canals, how a crank turned up the block sent a flood of cold mountain water through the carefully dug canals to water the neighborhood orchards. There were no irrigation canals in my arid orange-grove suburb.

In June, John Swenson was to leave for a two-year mission to Portugal, and he was terrified. His hands were stiff and cold. His tongue made dry, urgent forays into my mouth. Of course, I loved him, compulsively, the way one cannot help but love a drowning person.

Together, we took the tram to the top of Bridal Veil Falls where, like all the other soon-to-be missionaries and their teenage intendeds, we allowed ourselves to be gripped by the granite magnitude of these mountains and the cold, vast horizon of the eternities. He begged me to wait for him, to marry him someday, and, of course, I did not refuse, the way one cannot refuse a drowning person, or a riptide.

And yet I knew, sick inside, that I could not help but fail John Swenson, that all my promises would surely be broken. Which they were, sullenly, late that summer, on a stuffy and boredom-suffused August night, trying to break the monotony of my summer job in the office parks of my orange-grove suburb, my body frozen from eight hours under the industrial air-conditioning, not warming up one bit even in the backseat of a car, with an old high school classmate (how did I get there? by what strange gravity? so accidental and yet so inevitable?) who lifted up my shirt, while I hovered somewhere a few feet away, witnessing, not feeling. His name was Chris Ramos. His hands on my chest were evidence that I was not capable of keeping promises to John Swenson, chaste and lonesome in faraway Portugal, who would no longer want to marry me when he returned. It was then that the invisible weight of LeVar Royal's pearl necklace dropped from my neck.

As was specified in the rules, I went to the bishop's office the very next Sunday. The bishop's name was Grant Jensen. He was a short, square man, with a face like an owl's and a brushlike gray mustache. He was a professional Republican party pollster. I had worked for him the summer I was fifteen, in his little air-conditioned office in an industrial office park in my orange-grove suburb, printing out on transparencies, in shades of magenta, cyan, and green pie graphs charting voter opinions on gun control.

Bishop Jensen sat behind the great Formica-top desk in a high-back swivel chair. I sat next to the frosted window in a pool of afternoon light. Methodically, plainly, as was specified in the rules, I told him the events in the backseat of the car. While I confessed, I sat beside myself on the next chair, looking into the fuzzy light through the scalloped glass on the window.

I was eighteen. He was forty-three, maybe forty-four.

Bishop Jensen leaned back in the swivel chair. His lips began to move beneath his brushlike mustache.

"Let me tell you a story."

Bishop Jensen told me about a school bus driver who every day on his route traversed a hazardously steep hill and a set of railroad crossings. Up one side of the hills he piloted his bus, and then safely down the other, and across the tracks. Up one side, down the other, across the tracks. Every day, without incident.

One morning, with his bus full of schoolchildren, and running just a few minutes late, the driver felt his brakes fail just as he crested the hill. At the bottom of the hill, he saw a herd of goats in the road and the gates on the railroad tracks closing. Without a moment to spare, and yet without any panic, the bus driver took his foot off the gas, pressed the clutch, downshifted into first gear, and pulled on the emergency brake, bringing the bus full of children safely to rest just yards from the herd of goats and the railroad crossing.

A policeman who witnessed the incident rushed to the bus to see that everyone was okay.

"How did you do it?" the astonished policeman asked.

"Well, you see," said the bus driver, "every day when I drive my route and I bring the bus over the hill, I rehearse what it is that I should do if the brakes on the bus were to fail. In my mind, I imagine taking my foot off the gas, pressing the clutch, downshifting into first, pulling the emergency break, and bringing the bus full of children safely to stop just yards from the crossing gates. Today, when I had to put my plan into action, I was prepared."

"And you see," said my bishop Grant Jensen, "I want you to think of yourself as that bus driver. Practice in your mind the steps you will take to stop yourself if you feel your brakes failing, so that you can prevent this kind of situation from ever happening again. If you prepare, you will be able to stay in control."

I thanked Bishop Jensen for his counsel. I shook his hand, walked methodically down the church hallway to the parking lot, started my car, and drove home. Nothing inside me felt any better for confessing. In fact, what I felt in his office was what I felt in the backseat of the car that August night: nothing, nothing at all.

What I did not know how to say then was that the story was all wrong.

What if my body were not a bus with brakes that sometimes failed, hurtling me, thrilled and giddy, along with the onrush of some kind of sex?

What if, instead, I were just a doeling goat at the bottom of the hill, nosing about in the roadside blackberries, not entirely aware of my surroundings, not quick enough to know what to do when the brakeless bus of sex came hurtling down the hill toward me? Or what if I were just a child on the bus, and sex was like school, a compulsory education I never signed up for? Or what if I were like the policeman standing back and watching sex happen, a disastrous collision I had no power to stop? Or what if I were a mighty freight train steaming ahead toward my own horizon, and sex was the runaway bus that kept crossing my path?

What if the problem of sex always came uninvited, time and again, fleets of someone else's buses always losing their brakes, and me frozen in the roadway? What if it were always someone else's thrilling hurtle rushing headlong into the inert matter of my body?

It took a long time for me to realize that the story was all wrong, a long time to be able to ask these questions.

It was only after my mind had caught hold of all the corners of all the dim memories: when I was six, the face of the neighbor girl's father looming high above me; when I was thirteen, the neighbor boy catching me on the street in broad daylight on my walk home from cheerleading practice and forcing his grubby hands down my pants; what it was I had not been feeling in the backseat.

Then, slowly, I began to piece together an understanding of the problem sex had been, why it always felt inevitable and unchosen, something unavoidable to be avoided at all costs. I began to understand why my body felt like cold luggage, not at all like a pearl on a golden chain but more like a millstone, a constant reminder that my fate was to be drowned.

• • •

In the story I want to tell, there are no more drownings. I am waiting in the parking lot behind the church under the arc of a street lamp. I see my sixteen-year-old self leave the office of LeVar Royal. I see myself hurry down the steps, shoulders curled.

Would you like to go for a drive? I ask my sixteen-year-old self.

I hand her the keys.

My sixteen-year-old self gets into the front seat, takes the wheel, rolls down the window, and hollers, dark hair blowing.

We are driving in a muscle car, with shiny orange paint and an eight-cylinder engine. On the radio we hear the wailing guitars of the genius Wilson sisters of Heart, then witchy-wise Stevie Nicks.

We drive the long boulevards from the orange-grove hills down to the big industrial beaches bordered by power plants, concrete piers, giant piles of boulders, and long stretches of empty parking lot. The air is damp and salty and smells like mollusk.

We sit on the hood of the car and watch fires burn on the beach in great pits, then we walk out on the pier and watch the waves heave themselves on shore. Maybe we drink a Diet Coke.

Standing twenty feet above the heaving black ocean, not putting my arm around her, standing side by side, I tell my sixteen-year-old self:

It is not a doughnut.

It is not a rose.

It is not a plank of wood.

It is not a bus without brakes.

It is not a pearl on a golden chain, nor is it a millstone.

It is neither a fragile treasure nor a heavy burden.

It is nothing that can be damaged, taken, lost, or given away.

It is not an *it*.

You, your body, your *self*—you are not an object lesson.

You are an ancient spirit in a young body. You will make choices. You will make some good choices, and they will feel good in body and soul. You may also make some *moderately* bad choices, and they will leave you feeling a kind of confusion and loneliness. It might be that you do not choose some things that happen to you, and these are not your fault, and these too will leave you feeling alone and confused. You will learn to sort out your feelings. As you do, protect yourself. Be kind to yourself. It takes time.

How badly I want her to know that after many years of confusion, she will come home to a house she chose herself, with a man she chose herself, a man whose body does not menace, a man who does not dream of owning her. She will share a bed with him. She will go to bed wearing her own name. Two daughters in sweaty pajamas will dream sovereign dreams in their bedrooms down the hall. Doves will roost on the power lines, and hummingbirds will wet their beaks in the split fruit on her orange trees. The neighborhood roses will sit undisturbed atop their woody stems, fascicles tight with promise, or blowsy and exhausted from the expense of their perfume, unashamed.

On those nights, I want to tell her, if the stars align, and the girls stay asleep in their beds, and memory does not rattle at the windows, she will feel how sex feels. Like a state of levitation, like flying, like concentrating and letting go: she will feel . . . she will feel . . . she will feel. For a few seconds, she will be in another place: that place we reach when we come home to our bodies and find ourselves, for the first time, ready to travel.

This is what I want her to know, my sixteen-year-old Mormon girl self. But she cannot know it. Yet.

# 8

# files

I have not seen them, but I know they are there: millions upon millions of files entombed deep in the granite mountainside at the mouth of Little Cottonwood Canyon, just southeast of Salt Lake City. I have seen the narrow driveway that leads up from the canyon road to the parking lot carved into the mountainside; I have seen granite boulders the size of buildings split in half, a few neat drill marks remaining at the top where early last century our tireless ancestors dynamited a vault in the ancient gray canyon, a vault strong enough to withstand war, weather, even the end of time. I do not know whether the files are paper, computer tape, or digital, but I know they are there: millions upon millions of names rescued from census records and baptismal registries by Mormon genealogists, saved from oblivion, these names, the names of our ancestors. Wearing all white, we have carried their names on little paper slips through our holy temples. We have stepped into giant golden fonts resting on the back of twelve life-size golden statues of oxen, and we have been baptized, fully immersed in the shimmering turquoise water, maybe a dozen times in a row, for a dozen ancestors, in one day. By our labors, our ancestors are baptized again and married to each other once again, but this time for the eternities: beyond the scuttle of drying leaves, and the clouds of fruit flies, and the musky warmth of bodies in bed in the morning, they are sealed up against chaos and perdition. We are sealed to one another back through the generations. Our names are safe in the granite vault, and they will stay there until Jesus comes back and the stone is rolled away.

From end to end, everyone who has ever lived must be identified, baptized, and married again, either in the living flesh or by proxy, in one of our Mormon temples. Everyone who has ever lived—trillions upon trillions of them—their inscrutable names whirring before our eyes on reels of microfilm, or dissolving into paper powders in damp European sacristies, or dessicated like husks of scarab beetles and scattered out into the great deserts of the world, numberless as the sands of the beach or the stars of the skies, names of the dead forgotten even by the dead.

They are not forgotten by us. In time, the story goes, all the names will be fished out one by one by Mormon genealogists like my mother, who rise each morning in a thousand orange grove and alfalfa field suburbs across the American West, step into their sacred undergarments and modest workaday clothes, and with only a simple breakfast of milk and cereal, without even so much as a cup of coffee to steel them, set to work again at a task that will take the rest of time: the bureaucratic reorganization of chaos into order.

It used to hurt my head, when I was a kid, thinking about the impossibility of the work.

That's when my mother would smile, and rinse a dish in the sink, and explain that wonderful things would happen to hasten the work along, that in the millennium, someday, the temples would be open around the clock, that ancestors on the other side of the veil would provide unexpected assistance, that forbidden troves of records now hoarded by Communists and other unfriendly governments would soon fall open, that by unknown means the skies themselves would roll back like screens, as John the Revelator predicted, and great sources of knowledge would flash across them.

What is to stop a people who have sized up the infinite forest of human souls tangled and uprooted by the avalanche of time, and said, cheerfully, yes, we will sort it all out and have it stacked as neatly as cordwood by sundown.

What is to stop such a people?

When I was seventeen I drove with my parents up the I-15 from Orange County, California, to Provo, Utah, where I moved into a narrow little room in a college dormitory named after a Book of Mormon prophet. *Brigham Young University.* How I loved *Brigham Young University.* How many mornings had my mother roused me from bed at five a.m. for early morning seminary with the words of the BYU fight song: "Rise and shout! The Cougars are out!" How long I had looked forward to the day when I too could finally live among people who would understand me, to whom I would have to explain nothing, with whom I could wordlessly share knowing looks over mint chocolate-chip milk shakes in the very bosom of Zion. With my father and my mother at each elbow, I carried my boxes into Helaman Halls. In every room, girls from Mormon towns throughout the West—Mesa, Arizona; Burley, Idaho—were unpacking their boxes too. Well-scrubbed boys wearing short haircuts and long Levi's tossed a football on the perfectly manicured greens outside under the shadow of the twelve-thousand-foot Wasatch Mountains.

Surely *he* was here, I thought, as I looked across the dormitory lawns. I tried again to conjure in my head the shape of the man I would marry, as I had been doing whenever I was in large crowds of Mormons from the time I was thirteen or fourteen years old. So much on earth and in heaven depended on finding *him*, the one who would truly understand me and to whom I would have to explain nothing. And as my dormmates and I trooped around campus for orientation, I tried to ignore it—the sinking feeling in my belly. For all around me, crossing the quad between buildings named for apostles and prophets, from the Abraham O. Smoot Administration Building to the Harold B. Lee Library, climbing the steps from the George Albert Smith Fieldhouse, leaning on the glass counter at the Candy Jar outside the Varsity Theater, I saw so very many, very pretty Mormon girls, perfectly clear complected, lips perfectly glossed, long hair perfectly curled, girls who shimmered like the flanks of caramel-colored palominos in the sun. I looked down at my short fingernails and plain T-shirt tucked into baggy jeans; I reached up to touch my dark hair in its boyish cut. Panic seized me there in the lobby of the Ernest L. Wilkinson Student Center. There were so very many of *them*. How would *he* ever think to find *me*?

Our orientation tour finished in a classroom in the basement of the humanities building, where I took my place at a little student desk, still carrying the knot of panic in my belly. In through the door came a man of gentle mien with a crown of graying blond hair and useful-looking square hands. He set a few books down on the table at the front of the room, and with a clear, soft voice, introduced himself as Eugene England, a professor in the department of English. "Welcome to Brigham Young University." He smiled at us, his expression exquisitely kind.

Professor Eugene England did not carry himself in a way typical to Mormon men in authority. He did not wear a suit, white shirt, and tie, or speak with that Mormon mix of formality and sentiment. Instead, he wore a pressed denim shirt and khaki pants, and he moved about the classroom in a way that reminded me of my father in his stockinged feet in the kitchen on Saturday mornings, making hot cereal for his children.

On the chalkboard, Professor England wrote the following words, a verse from the Book of Mormon: "He denieth none that come unto him, black and white, bond and free, male and female; and he remembereth the heathen; and all are alike unto God, both Jew and Gentile." Then, he turned to watch us absorb the words into our minds. *All are alike unto God. Black and white. Male and female.*

I studied the round, outdoor-wizened face of Eugene England. I felt the knot of panic in my belly loosen and disappear. Deep inside my chest, a door opened. Light and oxygen flooded the room. And here it was again: that marvelous vision of an expansive and infinite universe, the dilation and contraction of time, all things at once present before God. But whereas, before, my cosmic Mormon vision had been colored by the dark tones of the end-times, I now saw it anew, here in this basement classroom in the BYU humanities building: "the glory of God was intelligence," as Joseph Smith wrote, "or, in other words, light and truth." I felt the universe unfurl in fractals of possibility, justice, and love, like the fronds of a great primeval fern. This thinking, this feeling—this was what we had been made for.

That fall and in the years that followed, I met other BYU professors who modeled for me what had yet been the great unmapped possibilities of Mormonism: a life of searching inquiry, fearless because we knew all truths pointed finally to the glory of God. I met seventy-year-old physicists who took me into their basement offices in the Carl F. Eyring Science Center, down among the giant particle accelerators, and patiently listened to an eighteen-year-old girl unbend the limbs of her mind. I met psychology professors who had served their missions among the Hopis fifty years before and who, with tongues chastened by the difficulty of the Hopi language, spoke as reverently of the rituals conducted in kivas as they did of our own Mormon temples. I met Utah-born women poets who lent me their own personal copies of Mary Wollstonecraft and Virginia Woolf. *Books*. For the first time in my life I learned how to find all the books I needed.

It was at Brigham Young University that I also found at the very heart of Mormonism something so rich and gentle, a variety of faith I had only glimpsed, only dreamed of from my Orange County suburb. But here they were—Mormon poets who had words to articulate the peculiar beauty of our world, Mormon historians who had been allowed to plunge freely into its archives until those archives were closed in the 1980s. In study rooms at the library, on walking trails in groves of box elder, black walnut, and horse chestnut trees south of campus, I met other young Mormon men and women like me, with searching minds, denim shirts, woolen socks, and clumsy haircuts, hungry for our legacy, hungry to learn this way of being Mormon in the world.

I was a sophomore when bombs started falling on Baghdad. It was January 1991, and Provo, Utah, was thousands upon thousands of miles from Iraq, but every night we gathered in the living rooms of our thin-walled BYU-approved apartments and watched round-the-clock CNN coverage of Desert Storm. Transfixing, it was, to me at least, and somehow perfectly coordinated—nighttime bombing raids, glowing green tracers and halos captured with night vision cameras, all scheduled for rebroadcast during peak nighttime viewing hours back in the United States. As the bombs fell, my roommates and their boyfriends sometimes cast a sidelong glance at the television screen, but generally proceeded as usual, coming and going, laughing loudly, the sound of hollow-core metal doors echoing through the apartment building halls.

How was one supposed to feel about the war? In my Honors classes, our professors guided us through classics of world religion—the *Upanishads*, the *Bhagavad Gita*, the *Tao Te Ching*. From small-town Arizona boys who had grown out their missionary haircuts and wore their hair tucked behind their ears—tempting the edges of the campus dress code—I gathered bits of information about President George H. W. Bush, Saddam Hussein, Saudi Arabia, oil revenues, and civilian targets. In the back row of my English classes, clear-eyed young women huddled together and trafficked in details about the antiwar march at the capital, the teach-in at the BYU campus Varsity Theater.

*What if war was wrong?* I wondered.

The scriptures routinely condemned violence. The Book of Mormon warned that pride led to the destruction of civilizations. Wasn't this a kind of pride: the callous delight we took in these nightly video-game-like images of human destruction?

I turned the idea over slowly in my mind. It was like nothing I had ever heard at home. Every Orange County Mormon I knew was an ardent conservative who accepted all wars as necessary sorties in the great Cold War battle against Communism: good versus evil, freedom versus unfreedom, a battle to the end of times. But what if the story was more complicated than it seemed? What if it was not so easy to trace the hand of God in history? What if the war was not as it had been presented as some unambiguously righteous endeavor but rather a story as much about ancient rivalries, human greed, and hunger for power, with innocent lives at stake? Such ideas seemed like an exotic species of wisdom from a civilization far away. But they too might be worth exploring, like the *Tao Te Ching*, or the *Bhagavad Gita*. This moral caution might be an element of intelligence a gentle and expansive Mormonism would find lovely and embrace.

Somehow I came into possession of a small peace-sign button. I turned it over in the palm of my hand, considered it carefully, and then pinned it to my shoulder bag. Soon it attracted the notice of roommates and their boyfriends, and then of the dwellers in the other thin-walled apartments up and down the halls.

One morning I opened the door of the apartment and found there freezing on the doorstep a six-pack of beer and a cassette tape—the chorus from the Cure song "Killing an Arab" recorded over and over and over again, thirty minutes straight. "Go ahead," said the note tucked in between the beer cans. "Have a drink. You're already there."

A few days later, on another cold February morning, I was walking from my apartment toward the groves at the south edge of campus. It was early, and I stepped carefully across the icy sidewalks. My hair was cut short in a pixie, and I was wearing thick black tights and a black and pink floral baby-doll dress I had sewn myself. My book bag with the peace-sign button hung on my shoulder.

A car pulled up behind me. Words hurled out the window: "Anti-Christ!"

The sting of shame spread across my shoulders—my first introduction to the martial edge of Mormon orthodoxy.

I kept walking. Ahead of me was school, the professors I loved, and the powerful ideas—all of them potentially sacred—from which I was fashioning my future.

I didn't look back.

So it happened that I was there at Brigham Young University just in time to witness a remarkable upwelling of Mormon feminism, a feminism that started very simply in basement classrooms with the idea that *all were alike unto God.* The University hired more women faculty in the late 1980s and 1990s, including Mormon women who had studied feminism and, finding nothing at its core incompatible with a just and loving God, dared to make it their own. One by one, Mormon feminist historians were publishing books reconstructing the lost worlds of early Mormon women, who, we learned, once commanded priesthood powers and forms of authority lost to women in the modern bureaucratic church. Mormon writers like Terry Tempest Williams fearlessly spoke out for the rural southern Utah "downwinders" who lived under plumes of atomic fallout, their lives and their wholeness knowingly sacrificed by the United States government, while Carol Lynn Pearson penned a play that dared to celebrate openly our hushed Mormon belief in God the Mother.

We were not the first Mormon feminists, to be sure. There were many others before us: early visionary Mormon women, pioneer widows who commanded their sick oxen to stand and carry their wagons across the plains, plural wives who traveled east from Utah in the 1870s to become medical doctors, women who continued to anoint and bless one another's bodies before confinement and childbirth, and in the 1970s and 1980s the courageous and embattled Mormons who campaigned for the Equal Rights Amendment. It was happening again in the early 1990s at Brigham Young

University, another wave of Mormon feminism. Together, in study groups and consciousness-raising meetings where Mormon women permitted only Mormon women to speak, we taught ourselves once again to tentatively (if sometimes clumsily) parse the grammar of Mormon feminism: *all are alike unto God*; *God is a Mother and a Father; Mormon women matter.*

Little did we then realize the powerful fears this grammar would disturb.

On August 6, 1992, at a gathering of Mormon liberals, artists, and intellectuals in Salt Lake City, Lavina Fielding Anderson, a sixth generation member of the Church, a feminist historian, and editor of the *Journal of Mormon History*, disclosed the existence of the Strengthening the Members Committee, "an internal espionage system" organized by Church elders in the 1980s to keep files on members perceived to be critical of the Church. *Files.* It was another set of files, but unlike the ones up Little Cottonwood Canyon, these were organized not for the salvation of the dead but for the surveillance of the living. BYU professor and renowned Mormon intellectual Eugene England, speaking on the same panel as Lavina, reacted immediately by denouncing the Strengthening the Members Committee and calling for its dissolution.

Church spokesman Don LeFevre confirmed the existence of the committee the following week. He explained to newspapers that the committee "receives complaints from church members about other members who have made statements that 'conceivably could do harm to the church,' " then "pass the information along to the person's ecclesiastical leader" to "provide local church leadership with information designed to help them counsel with members who, however well-meaning, may hinder the progress of the church through public criticism." Another Mormon elder compared the Strengthening the Members Committee to a kind of "clipping service" that tracked critical writings, including letters to the editors, published by Church members.

On August 22, 1992, the First Presidency of the Church issued a statement defending the Strengthening the Members Committee, citing instructions from Joseph Smith in 1839, when he was imprisoned by the state of Missouri during the "Mormon War," that a record should be made of "sufferings and abuses put on" Mormons and the "names of all persons that have had a hand in their oppressions."

That same summer, Church members Paul and Margaret Merrill Toscano founded the Mormon Alliance to counter what they described as growing patterns of spiritual intimidation within the institutional Mormon Church. In the fall of 1992, Lavina Fielding Anderson and Mormon feminist Janice Merrill Allred formed a special Mormon Alliance subcommittee to document instances of spiritual intimidation and abuses of ecclesiastical authority within the institutional Church, while Eugene England made a public apology for denouncing the Strengthening the Members Committee, which he admitted he had first incorrectly thought to be composed of regular church employees but which, in fact, included some of the highest ranking members of the Church leadership, the Quorum of the Twelve Apostles.

In the spring of 1993, Lavina Fielding Anderson published in the Mormon journal *Dialogue* an article describing a growing pattern of "spiritual and ecclesiastical abuse" in the Church, wherein members critical of church authoritarianism were being subjected to ecclesiastical investigation and their church membership threatened.

On May 18, 1993, Church leaders identified the objects of surveillance, when Boyd K. Packer, a member of the Quorum of the Twelve Apostles, delivered a speech to the Mormon All-Church Coordinating Council declaring that the three greatest "dangers" to the Church were the "gay-lesbian movement," "the feminist movement," and the "so-called scholars or intellectuals."

In June 1993, Brigham Young University fired Cecilia Konchar Farr, a feminist literary critic and my mentor. Within months, several other feminist BYU professors announced their resignations from the faculty.

Beginning on September 14, 1993, with the disfellowshipping of Mormon feminist Lynne Kanavel Whitesides, the Church embarked on the serial excommunication of prominent feminists and intellectuals, a group now known as the September Six.

One of the six was Lavina Fielding Anderson, who was excommunicated on September 23, 1993, at a church court held in her local ward house. Others included Paul Toscano, Mormon feminist Maxine Hanks, and renowned Mormon historian D. Michael Quinn.

Lavina Fielding Anderson continued to attend her Salt Lake City ward each week. No word was spoken of her excommunication. She was not allowed to take the sacrament. She was allowed, though, to play the piano in Relief Society, the only church calling permitted of a nonmember.

In 1995, Lavina and the Mormon Alliance published a first volume of case reports documenting more than twenty cases over the last decade in which tithe-paying Mormon church leaders, including bishops, Sunday School teachers, missionaries, and Scout troop leaders had been convicted of sexually abusing children. Much of the sexual abuse Lavina documented had taken place in Mormon ward houses, campouts, and prayer meetings, often with the knowledge and inaction of other church leaders. Some parents of abused children had been excommunicated for "embarrassing the Church."

In 1995, Lavina asked her stake president what she could

do in order to be rebaptized. He responded that she needed to stop thinking that "the General Authorities could ever do wrong."

On May 9, 1995, Janice Merrill Allred, coeditor of the Mormon Alliance Case Reports and a Mormon feminist theologian who had condemned the abuse of children within the Church, was summoned to her local ward house for a disciplinary court. She usually walked to church, but she was on crutches, and so was driven by her sister, Mormon feminist and Mormon Alliance cofounder Margaret Merrill Toscano. Lavina Fielding Anderson walked Janice to the door of the court. Behind closed doors, Janice was excommunicated by a council of twelve men.

On June 5, 1996, Brigham Young University fired Mormon feminist English professor Gail Turley Houston. She had written an article in an off-campus student newspaper revealing that she had prayed to both Heavenly Father and Heavenly Mother.

In 1997, Lavina Fielding Anderson published the third volume of case reports presenting essays on the fates of distressed Brigham Young University students, wayward missionaries, gay and lesbian Mormons, and Mormon intellectuals who had been fired or excommunicated for their scholarship.

In 1997, the leadership of the Church of Jesus Christ of Latter-day Saints embarked on the beginnings of what would be a ten-year campaign to eradicate the possibility of same-sex civil marriage rights for gays and lesbians in the Western United States by making a $500,000 donation to a defense of marriage amendment initiative campaign in Alaska. Over the next three years, the Church mobilized money and resources in support of anti-same-sex marriage efforts in Hawaii and California.

Mormon feminist and Mormon Alliance cofounder Margaret Merrill Toscano was excommunicated on November 30, 2000.

In 2003, Lavina Fielding Anderson spoke about her excommunication at a public gathering of one thousand people in Salt Lake City. "Mormonism is my world. It's my language, my people, my music, my history, even my leaders," she said. "My God is the Mormon God. I'm not rejecting Mormonism. I'm not trying to reform Mormonism. I am trying to remind Mormons of the truth and power and glory of its paradoxical assertion of absolute freedom and absolute love, a paradox that is reconciled in Jesus Christ."

During this decade, I was twenty, twenty-two, twenty-three. The Church I was born into, baptized into, raised up in, the Church of my grandmothers and great-grandmothers, the Church I had attended as many as twelve hours a week every week of my life, and tithed to, my Church had declared me a double enemy. Not the multilevel marketers who used Mormon membership records to defraud their fellow Saints, or the CIA intelligence experts devising legal justifications for torture, nor the pedophile bishops who cost the Church millions of tithing dollars in legal judgments; not untruth, not fear, not greed. But me, and the others like me I met while a student at Brigham Young University—a small cohort of Mormon liberals, trying to find or make a place for ourselves within a tradition we loved.

I graduated from BYU, without a husband, returned my diploma in protest, and left Utah for a PhD program in Los Angeles. Sometimes I dizzily wandered the palm-lined concrete canyons of the city, or hid away in cool library corridors, or wept in the back row of Black churches on Easter Sunday, or canned soup at the great Mormon-owned welfare cannery on Eleventh Street in East Los Angeles. On Saturday nights, I put on my black cha-cha heels and wore my heartbreaks like invisible ruby earrings, glinting in the dark. On Sunday mornings, I got up and went to church. I kept going, I kept going. I sang hymns and taught Sunday School classes, no matter how desolate I felt inside. Sometimes I found refuge among the Korean- and Spanish-language Mormon congregations of Los Angeles, Mormon places unpenetrated by the purge. Sometimes I visited a gray-haired waitress at Canter's Jewish deli in the Fairfax district, she who brought me my first plate of *matzah brei*, and in a spirited mix of English, Yiddish, Spanish, and Hungarian told me how the Holocaust had driven her family from Hungary to Mexico and taught me the world-shaping scope of other purges. Sometimes I marched among thousands of student protestors or striking hotel workers, and I sat down in city intersections to be arrested. Whenever I sat down, I sat down as a Mormon feminist mourning her own exile from the Church of her ancestors, though to look at me no one could tell.

Not a word about the firings or excommunications passed between me and my parents—not about the teachers and the writers I loved, or what had happened to them or the great sadness I felt or the martial edge of Mormon orthodoxy I had experienced. Because orthodox Mormonism was still their home. It was their four walls, their seven days, their twenty-four hours. What could I have possibly said that would not have been simply a source of shame and disappointment to them? What could I have possibly said that could have been to them more than just evidence of my own personal failings? Perhaps I wanted to protect them from shame. Perhaps I wanted to protect myself from feeling the brunt of their shame. In any case, we did not speak about any of it. Nor did my brother, or my sisters, really—each of us consumed privately, in our own way, with the hammering out of the kinds of Mormons we would be, with the serving of missions, the finding of Mormon spouses, the launching of careers, the subduing of the shadows that manifest in every life. We each wrestled in those years with our shadows, but we did not speak much about them. Once in a while, I might mention the Mormon purge of feminists and intellectuals to my fellow PhD students, especially the small and enchanting crew of dark-haired, cigarette-smoking Marxists I loved, each one of them being in some way an exile from their own ancestral contexts. During breaks in our literary theory seminars, they would listen, nod in solidarity, then scrub their butts out under their heels before we dutifully returned to Heidegger and Althusser. But aside from my books, the place I felt safest was on Sunday evenings in the kitchen of my Utah-born grandmother. She had moved to Los Angeles during the Great Depression, and when she arrived, strangers on the streetcars reached out to feel her head for horns. Now widowed, in her late seventies, living in a Los Angeles suburb, she took me in and asked me no questions. We shared the comfort of plain and buttery little dinners, her deep lonesomeness holding hands with my own. Late Sunday nights, back in my tiny studio apartment, I put my head on my bed and cried and cried, and demanded that God lift the fear and hurt from my heart, then fell asleep, exhausted, and dreamed of my great-grandmothers dressed in white.

Though I spoke few words about it to the people with whom I shared my everyday life, during this decade, Mormons like me found ourselves in the grip of a terrible turn in Mormon history, in the grip of a fear provoked in part by the strength of our Mormon feminist vision: a fear of the full, glorious, strange, and difficult humanity of our Mormon past; a fear of women who openly claimed the power of a Heavenly Mother; a fear of mothers and fathers who refused to sacrifice their children to protect the public image of the Church; a fear of our own gay and lesbian relatives who refused the confines of the closet. *Exile.* It took a decade to come to terms with the fact that the Church we loved had declared us its enemies. And slowly the immensity of our work dawned on us, as we realized it would take a superhuman strength born of stubbornness, anger, desperation, and love to hold on to the faith of our ancestors. Some of us stopped talking about our thoughts and feelings for the sake of maintaining our peace with husbands, wives, parents, and brothers and sisters, for the sake of keeping our homes, our seats on wooden pews in familiar ward houses. Some of us dropped out of Mormon life, refusing to reveal our ancestral pasts even to our natural-born children. Some of us hung on, in daylight, in darkness, to the tenuous and tender threads of a Mormon exile community. We hid out in intermountain suburbs. We pulled ourselves back across the plains to college towns and big East Coast cities. We gathered by the rivers of the internet and laughed and wept when we remembered Zion. From Boise, Mesa, Los Angeles, from Boston and Philadelphia, we lived the whole series of excommunications and firings. And we too kept files, evidence of all that had happened, was happening in this great and terrible turn. Through the years, I saved clandestine copies of all the documents pertaining to Cecilia's firing and Lavina's excommunication; a copy of the 1993 "three greatest enemies" speech; copies of newspapers articles and Mormon Alliance case reports. I kept files because I needed evidence to substantiate the fear I felt inside, evidence I might need if I had to go into a closed room with twelve men and defend myself.

We exiles too compiled files as if our lives depended on it.

But files do not make for an actual life.

For years I told myself that if I were a better Mormon, if I had milder thoughts, a tamer spirit—if I were just *better*, God would turn it all around and reward me with a good Mormon husband, someone who would understand not only our common faith but also the challenges it entailed for women like me. One Sunday, when I was twenty-five years old, I found myself in a chapel full of unmarried Mormon women who also believed that if they were better Mormons, with milder thoughts, and a tamer spirit, God would reward them with good Mormon husbands too. Most of the women, they were nearing forty.

*What should I do?* I asked myself. *What should I do?* I asked the white-haired bishop of my Mormon singles ward. His name was Tom Anderson. He was a big, broad-shouldered man, a man who as the leader of a congregation of single Los Angeles Mormons had heard the human story in all of its predictable variety. He invited me to his house in Los Angeles one Sunday afternoon. Pink and red roses bloomed in the front yard. We sat down at the dining room table.

"We often ask God over and over again what it is we

should do," Bishop Anderson said. He smiled. "But sometimes we just have to do and seek God in the process."

And so I *did*. I did, and I did.

I did go to a party one night in Venice Beach. And I did see a freckle-faced, blue-eyed Jewish man wearing a surfer's watch walk in the front door. And I did like him. Oh, how I did like him. My heart said, "He looks like home to me."

On our first date, we listened to country music and drove around nighttime Los Angeles in his oversize white GMC Jimmy.

On our second date, David and I went skateboarding in Venice Beach. "You're in love," a passing stranger hollered at us.

*Yes, you are right*, I thought.

Wherever David was, I noticed, there was always food, music, and people. In his Venice Beach apartment, salt air wafted through the open windows, and dub reggae or punk rock or opera played on the stereo. He bustled and spun about the kitchen, soaking exotic dried mushrooms, roasting peppers, and flipping them in hot pans. He listened and held my hand when I talked about feeling sad sometimes and all the reasons I felt sad, and he did not wince—visibly at least—when God came into the conversation. After all, he was Jewish. He understood what it felt like to have God in the conversation, how it felt to belong to a people, and how it felt to be the only one of your kind in the room. We fell in love during long study sessions at Venice Beach coffeehouses and teaching assistants' union meetings. The week our union went on strike, David signed up for every picket shift, and he ferried water around to each of the picket sites in his big white truck. "This," I said to myself, "is a man who could make it across the plains."

One jasmine-scented spring Los Angeles night, we found ourselves sitting on a curb outside a friend's wedding reception.

"You know, we're going to get married," I told him.

He smiled, shook his head, looked at his feet, said, "Slowly, slowly."

I was not deterred.

"And this Mormon thing, it's not going away. You know that, right?"

"Yes," he said. "I know."

Doctrine teaches that only couples married in Mormon temples reach the highest levels of heaven. To my family, my choosing to marry David would mean that I was choosing *not* to be with them in heaven. But for me, choosing David meant placing my trust in a God bigger than doctrine. It meant choosing my joy, my best friend, my chance to create a family, choosing all of these as indivisible elements of my own spiritual well-being. It meant marrying a man who saw no enmity in me, a man who would never put me on trial or audit my heart for heresy. Certainly even a Mormon like me deserved that much in a marriage.

So I did. I married him. I said, *Yes.* Like the glass crushing under my bridegroom's heel, I gave way and I said, *Yes, God, do with me what you will.*

David and I finished our degrees. We moved halfway across the country, to my first job as a professor, into a little two-bedroom wood-frame house on a pecan tree-lined street near the university. My files, we brought them with us.

And exile cast no shadow over our marriage.

One humid summer morning, six months pregnant with our first child—a daughter—I set to work turning our office into her bedroom. *Room*. There was not enough room. I boxed up surplus books, dragged old furniture out on the lawn, then turned to face my files, taking up too much space in the room I now needed for my daughter. I sat down in a puddle of light on the wooden floor, my belly giant in my lap. I opened the file cabinet drawer. I read all the memos and clippings again, reviewed all the hurt and the evidence, wept again, and again, and rehearsed my case one final time. Then, from the giant stack of files, I pulled out a few pieces of paper I wanted to share with my daughter, things I wanted her to remember, things I needed her to carry forward. The rest of it—my files, my carefully prepared defense case, the evidence of fearful treachery, the speech that named me an enemy among my own people, the bitterness of exile I wanted no part of her memory—all of this, I heaved and toted out to the garbage.

During the exile years, I wore my faith under my clothing, threads of stubborn refusal and hopeful determination, bound tight about my rib cage. During the exile years, I lived within my faith like a narrow pillar of light: above me, my grandmother, my great-grandmother, a hundred great-grandmothers dressed in white; above them God the Mother, God the Father. Every month a woman came to visit me from the local Mormon congregation. Her name was Sister Bryson. She had wide hips and puffy hands, wore pastel-colored scarves, and talked with a soft Mormon accent that made my heart ache. When my daughter Ella was born, Sister Bryson filled my fridge with creamy casseroles. She talked to me in a womanly way about how exhausting it was, the breast-feeding, for she knew, having nursed three, four, five children herself. Back in the small Arizona Mormon outpost where she grew up, she would tell me, her mother pointed out the cows standing around and lying down in the irrigated pastures, explaining that that's how exhausting nursing was, and so it was okay just to lie down and take it easy through all the nursing months. Once in a while, as we sat on my couch, my eyes welled up with tears of fear and loneliness. "You'll be fine," Sister Bryson would say, sensing my fear that I had done it all wrong, read wrong, thought wrong, loved wrong, married wrong, lost my way. "You'll be fine," she would say, resting her hand on mine, "because you are searching for truth, and truth is what matters."

During the exile years, every few months I received

a newsletter from the Mormon Alliance. It came, I knew, directly from the hand of Lavina, a woman with wide hips and puffy hands. There was always a little heart in blue ink penned in above my address label. *Love.* How I loved the blue inked heart that came to my mailbox from the hand of Lavina. Standing on the front lawn of my safe house in a college town miles away from Salt Lake City, I pressed my lips to the heart. During a long decade in exile, that heart and my visits from Sister Bryson were church to me.

I do not know for sure, but I suspect that I may very well have my own file in the Strengthening the Members Committee storeroom in one of the great church skyscrapers in downtown Salt Lake City. I am, after all, a Mormon feminist, scholar, and writer.

I can guess about how thick the file is now, for I have furnished it myself. I have been writing and publishing since I was eight years old, when my first Christmas poem appeared in the *Friend*, a glossy Mormon children's magazine. I think of the minor exposés and navel-gazing essays I published in the underground student newspaper at Brigham Young University, and the raw feminist poetry that leaked from me in my college years. I think of the speech I gave when I returned my diploma at a press conference after Cecilia's firing in May 1993. I don't think I have a transcript, but that's okay: it's probably there in my file.

Maybe the diploma I sent back to Brigham Young University is there too. Or the articles and poems and stories I wrote and published in Mormon liberal magazines during those early years in exile, writing full of images of bruised and occluded Mothers and burning sacred groves. Maybe too there are the one or two scholarly essays I wrote about Mormon feminism during the exile years, only on assignment, clenching my jaw and dragging myself through fear to write what I know.

Of course, if I have a file, it will soon contain the very words I am now typing into my computer, *click-click-click-click.* Surely by the time you are reading them these words will have been clipped and summarized.

Here, let me sum it up myself:

*All are alike unto God: male and female, black and white, gay and straight.*
*God is a Mother and a Father.*
*Mormon women matter.*

Sometimes over the last few years, when I have felt tired or out of sorts or very alone, I have imagined cheerful, tireless clerks, men of thinning pates who wake each morning in the alfalfa field suburbs of the intermountain West and call their wives "mother." I have imagined them, the agents of an infinite regime of spiritual surveillance, as a second audience to every insignificant email. *Click-click-click-click-click-click.*

For what is to stop the everyday Mormon people who, without so much as a cup of coffee to bolster their assurance, expend days tirelessly tracking through thickets of print the scent trail of the beast called "apostasy"? What is to prevent everything we write—the actual human dimensions of our living faith, our own unvarnished histories, records of our searching hungers—from being used as evidence against us? If we have already been judged to be the enemies of our own Church, what keeps us from excommunication, from having our names removed from the safekeeping of the granite vaults in the mountains, from the company of our ancestors, made dead to our own dead?

Mercy, only mercy keeps us.

*Click-click-click-click-click-click.*

# 9

# sealed portion

[Here are parts of the story I do not want to tell.

But I will for you, wayward Mormon boy or girl. I will for you, girl seeking.

Because our stories are not told in sacred books. They are not told over the pulpit. They are not told by the prophets.

No one says: I felt my church turn away from me, and it was a kind of death to me.

No one says: I drove into the desert. I wandered around the city in the dark. I was alone and it was cold and inside me was desolation.

No one says: I sat in the hotel lobby bathroom, my rib cage wracked with sobs, until a stranger, insistent, knocked at the stall door, handing me a Kleenex and urging me to be strong.

No one says: when my family treated me as a stranger, I preferred the company of strangers, and I walked among strangers and what did I find but God in every one of their faces.

No one says: I broke rules, I broke rules, I broke rules—I broke all the rules. That one. And that one. And that one too. Yes. I did.

No one says: I lay on the floor of the Venice Beach apartment and Parliament Funkadelic was on the record player and my friend and I, we looked at the ceiling, and I waved the smoke from the air with the back of my hand, and when he asked, "Help me understand what Mormonism means to you?" I said, "it is my first language, my mother tongue, my family, my people, my home; it is my heart, my heart, my heart."

No one says any of these things. But they should.

Because no one should be left to believe that she is the only one.

No one should be left to believe that she is the only Mormon girl who walked alone into the dark. No one should be left to feel like she is the only one broken and seeking.]

# 10

# pioneer day

How is it we come through the most difficult miles? Do we come silent or singing? Do we come in company, or do we come alone? Are we all alone on the open plains under starlit skies, all alone with the cooing owls in the dark of early morning? Our ancestors, our grandmothers, will their spirits take pity on us?

I am a descendant of Mormon pioneers. My great-great-great grandmother Lucy Evalina Waterbury Wight crossed the plains from Council Bluffs, Iowa, to the Salt Lake Valley with her husband and one-year-old daughter Rachel in 1852. She was nineteen years old. Lucy was born in 1833 in the cold northern reaches of St. Lawrence County, New York. One winter afternoon, when Lucy was twelve, her father left her to watch over her dying mother and two younger siblings while he went to the neighbors for help. Charlotte Post Waterbury died, and Lucy, terrified, could not bear to stay in the house with her mother's body. She bundled up herself and her two siblings and trudged out into the deepening dark of the afternoon. Three years later, just fifteen years old, she would arrive alone at the Mormon settlement of Nauvoo, Illinois. How she came through those miles, no one knows.

My great-great-grandmother Rachel Jane Wight was one year old when her mother, Lucy Waterbury, and her father, Stephen Wight, pulled the family's few possessions in a handcart from Iowa to Utah. Rachel grew up in Brigham City, a town named for the prophet Brigham Young, with her father, her mother, two sister-wives, and seventeen other siblings. In 1864, her father sent back across the Missouri River for a piano, only the second to be brought to Brigham City. Rachel taught herself to play the piano as hornets buzzed under the house eaves on hot summer afternoons. At seventeen, she married John Thorpe, a Yorkshire-born Mormon convert, and returned with him to his family home among the box elder trees in the Malad Valley of Idaho.

Rachel Wight Thorpe died in April 1884, three weeks after the birth of my great-grandmother, her third child, Rachel Maude. John Thorpe could barely stand to look at his infant daughter. Maude was sent off to be raised by her grandmother, Elizabeth Sims Thorpe, a toothless and gossipy midwife from the ancient forests of Derbyshire, who had at great trouble insisted on carrying a trunk of teas with her from England and across the plains. Little Maude wandered in and out of the dimming eyesight of her grandmother, wearing a dirty dress and dragging around a bottle of milk with a rubber nipple until she was five or six years old. At nine, she was sent back to live in the shadow of her father's bitterness. Sitting out by the family well one summer evening, Maude saw a girl with long black hair in a white dress come across the field and through the gate. She spoke to the girl. She asked her if she were a friend of her older sisters Florence or Minnie, but the girl did not answer. Frightened, my great-grandmother ran into the house. She told her father what this girl—this "personage," as my grandmother described her—looked like. John Thorpe told Maude to go to bed and went outside. When he came back into the house, he called for my great-grandmother. "Lass," he said, "that was your mother you saw." John Thorpe showed Rachel Maude Thorpe to a trunk containing her mother's clothes and told her she could have them.

How Maude made her way to Garland, Utah, no one knows, but it was there one night outside the great sugar beet factory built by the Mormon Church for the benefit of Zion that she met my great-grandfather, a migrant beet worker named David Dorton. She married him in the upper room of a local furniture store, settled in a little house across the street from the factory, and had six children. Their youngest was my grandmother America Pearl Dorton, born in April 1917. For a few years, Pearl grew up in an oven-warmed kitchen, yeast-start on the windowsill, playing at her mother's feet as Maude rushed to get lunch on the table for noontime boarders from the factory. But bad times came for the industry: overproduction, declining prices, white fly. The Dorton family scattered out from Garland and tried to outrun failure. The older boys, D. J. and Bill, hopped freight to find work on the ranches of Montana, and the older sisters, Vera and Deon, left for the cities.

During the cold bottom years of the Great Depression, my great-grandfather abandoned my great-grandmother Maude, and grandmother Pearl in a lonesome little sugar beet factory town in western South Dakota. The sugar mill where he was working failed, and the marriage followed. Left to fend for themselves, marooned hundreds of miles from their lovely Deseret, Maude and Pearl filled their abandoned house with roomers and boarders. It was tough sledding, as my grandmother used to say. One day my great-aunt Vera came back from the cities in her four-seater Chevrolet. "We're here to get you," she told them. "You can't go on like this." There was only room enough for Maude and Pearl to bring their few clothes in paper suitcases. Not even room, my grandmother remembered, to bring the old doll she played dinner with under the apple trees in happier days at her childhood Utah home.

• • •

*You can't go on like this.*

For years, I cried every time I set foot in a Mormon ward house. Crying out of fear and anger and loneliness and misunderstanding. Crying that the Church had punished women like me, people like me, leaving us exiled among our own. Still, I kept bringing myself back, sobbing in the pews, nursing my baby daughter Ella to keep her quiet. Even after services, when the dark-suited bishop would materialize to shake my hand, I would stand there in the foyer with tears coming down my cheeks. Ridiculous. Is this how God wanted me to spend my Sundays, lonesome among my own people, obvious, angry, and humiliated?

*You can't go on like this.* How badly I wanted to belong as I had when I was a young Mormon girl, to be simply a working part in the great Mormon plan of salvation, a smiling exemplar of our sparkling difference. But instead I found myself a headstrong Mormon woman staking out her spiritual survival at a difficult point in Mormon history. "You'll leave the Church," non-Mormon friends would sometimes confide, patting me gently on my hand. They could see the depths of my anguish. "You don't deserve to belong here," said conservative voices in the Church. *No, no, no*, I pushed back, in my heart, in my prayers. How to pull myself out of this desolation?

*You can't go on like this*, I told myself. And You can't possibly want me to feel this way, I demanded of God. God didn't argue. Forced to choose between my nostalgia for the faith of my childhood and my dignity as an adult, I put down the doll and drove away.

Who watches over us when we go? Who remembers our names when we disappear from home? Who hears the absence of our voices? Who misses the sound of our stories?

My grandmother Pearl was always my refuge. For my brother and sisters and I, Pearl was the one who sewed our back-to-school outfits, scratched our backs, and stood over the stove stirring tapioca, milk, and sugar as long as it took to make pudding.

Late in her life, my grandmother sat down at the kitchen table of her house in Los Angeles to write her own life story. She remembered how it was in Garland, her small Utah hometown, how her own parents kept a coffee pot on the stove, and how people were not as strict about rules or doctrine, but still taught the gospel as it should be taught, and who else were they to be, anyway, but Mormons? Who else in all the world were we supposed to be?

My grandmother remembered the day she turned eight years old, the age at which children are baptized into the Mormon Church. Pearl was living with her mother Maude in Salt Lake City. On the morning of her birthday, with her mother sick in bed, Pearl set out by herself to walk the long blocks down South Temple Avenue, past the mansions of prophets, seers, and revelators, governors and bankers, homes where her mother cooked and cleaned for a living, to present herself for baptism at the Mormon Tabernacle downtown. Alone, she changed into a homely little handmade one-piece suit of white clothing and stepped into the baptismal font, a majestic golden bowl resting on the back of twelve golden oxen, representing the gathered tribes of Israel. A stranger took her in his arms, lowered her beneath the water, and raised her up again. Pearl always remembered the terrible forlornness of that day, sidewalks wet and littered with elm pollen, her Dutch bangs under a little crocheted cap, her long and lonely walk.

A bone-soaking sense of loneliness pervades so much of my Mormon pioneer history: dead mothers, sick mothers, missing mothers, daughters marooned in loneliness, daughters trudging on. But there is to me in the story of Maude and Pearl an undeniable sense of warmth and loyalty as well. Scattered out from Zion by forces beyond their control, my great-grandmother and her daughters clung together and cared for one another without fail. When my grandmother turned eighteen, she and my great-grandmother again packed their few things in paper suitcases and boarded the train for Los Angeles. What a terrible mistake, my grandmother thought, to leave Zion for this great chaotic city, to dwell so far from the familiar company of other Mormons, in a place where strangers sometimes rubbed her head to feel for horns. But my grandmother had also learned a few things about survival. Maude and Pearl settled into a tiny apartment with her sister Edna and brother-in-law Alme, who worked at the local Firestone tire plant. Pearl got up early and took the red car, memorized the names of the downtown city streets, and found a job at a blouse factory. Alme bought her a bathing suit at Woolworth's. She met my grandfather Frank, a kind and churchless Los Angeles Basque, who made Pearl a home under the palm trees in a working-class suburb and helped her support and care for her mother until the day she died. This was their triumph: that unlike the generations of pioneer mothers and daughters before them, Maude and Pearl came all the lonely miles together.

My grandmother married outside the faith and never held what others might consider an important church assignment or calling. She did not receive her temple endowments until she was well into her widowhood. She was unimpressed by hierarchy and utterly averse to harshness or cruelty. Hers was a tender Mormonism carried in the bone, a faith forged in the small acts of care that stand between family survival and oblivion.

During my years away from church, it is the Mormonism of my grandmothers that keeps me company: their brave and forlorn walks, their small acts of care, their loneliness companioning mine. The impetus of faith. The mystery that brings us across the empty distances.

• • •

When my daughter Ella is almost two years old and my second daughter, Rosa, curled up in my belly, my grandmother Pearl makes her own final crossing, passing away after a long struggle with dementia.

Standing on the driveway of the funeral home back in Orange County, six months pregnant, I worry that because my life has taken an unorthodox path, I will not be invited in to help dress my grandmother's body. When observant Mormons die, their bodies are dressed for burial in sacred vestments: white undergarments embroidered with small symbols commemorating vows of obedience and devotion, long white dresses for women and white suits and ties for men, and embroidered green aprons. Mormon family members and friends dress their bodies ourselves, partly out of modesty, not wanting to reveal the private aspects of our faith to outsiders, and partly as a final act of love and service. I worry that I will have to spend the time staring at dusty silk plants and electric candelabra bulbs in the funeral home lobby, just as I had sat outside the Mormon temple during the weddings of my two sisters and my brother.

My worry is for nothing. When my sisters arrive—wearing giant sunglasses, toting oversize leather bags, perfectly arrayed in the sumptuous exhaustion of their grief—my mother leads us all into the mortuary dressing room.

Everything inside is pink, from the seashell pink wallpaper to the mauve couch to the pink box of pink tissues resting on the faux mahogany side table.

The body of my grandmother rests on a gurney under a white drape.

The funeral home manager withdraws with a gentle, knowing smile. (He too is Mormon.) We four living women stand in a circle and bow our heads.

"Help us to do this service for Pearl," my mother prays.

In her death, Grandma becomes just *Pearl.* Alive, she ruled our worlds, a full five feet four inches looming above us, queenly in her ranking. Now her spirit stands next to us, like another sister positioned at the long bathroom mirror on a warm June Sunday morning before church, arranging her bangs in the glass. She cannot reach the buttons on her own dress. So we will button it for her.

My mother has brought new undergarments and new temple clothes—dress, apron, stockings, slippers—all in their plastic packages. She has also brought a pair of scissors to help us prepare the clothing so we can slip it over her limbs and around her body. We stand around the gurney. I allow my mother and sisters to position themselves near her head and shoulders, out of respect and deference: they have been through the temple and will know how to dress my grandmother in her ceremonial clothing, as I do not. I will tend to my grandmother's feet and legs.

My mother draws the sheet down to my grandmother's shoulders.

"Hello, Pearl."

What a relief it is to see her body. I am startled to feel so relieved, but I do. It is blindingly plain that she is no longer there. Her body is shiny, dry, all surfaces, like a beautiful piece of paper.

Since the time that we were small children, we have rehearsed the Mormon belief that the human body is a transitory habitation for a spirit being that existed before this life and will exist afterward. We rehearsed the parable of embodiment in small church classrooms, around the family dinner table: here is the fleshy, animate hand—here is the cotton gardening glove—at birth the hand enters the glove—at death the glove is peeled from the living hand and laid out on the table.

When she was alive, I never saw my grandmother naked. Now I see that she has parts like mine, hips like mine, hair like mine. I reach for her hands. I welcome the feel of the pads on her thumbs, worn softly impermeable against the steady press of paring knives in the kitchen. I welcome the sight of her legs, uncurled from the infantile palsies of her long decline into dementia.

I slip my arm under her legs and help my sister slide her sacred undergarments over her bare hips. I hold her bare feet in my hands, her toes contorted by four decades of fashionable women's shoes. I ease the white stockings over her feet, rolling the nylon above the calves. I put on the white slippers and gently pat her feet.

I step back to let my mother and sisters put her ceremonial clothing in place.

"You look beautiful, Pearl," my sister says.

My mother pulls the sheet back up to her chin.

What will I leave my own daughters, my own granddaughters? What stories will accompany them across the miles they will travel in their lifetimes? For their sakes, finally, I decide to stop feeling like a bad daughter in my own tradition. For their sakes, I decide I must make and tell my own version of the Mormon story.

I start with Pioneer Day. It was on July 24, 1847, after crossing fifteen hundred miles of rattlesnake-infested and sagebrush-choked plains that Brigham Young, stricken with Rocky Mountain spotted fever, raised himself upon one elbow from his carriage sickbed, gazed down at the Salt Lake Valley, and pointed a finger: "It is enough. This is the right place. Drive on." Mormons around the world celebrate this memory every July 24 on Pioneer Day, our one and only Mormon holiday, the birthday of our lovely Deseret.

I have photographs of myself as a little girl on Pioneer Day in a calico bonnet and ankle-grazing skirt sewn by my grandmother. In the photographs, my two sisters and I stand bonneted astride our Huffy scooters in a suburban California cul-de-sac. Now I have a yellow eyelet bonnet for four-year-old Ella, freckle faced and irrepressible, and a white bonnet with red and blue stars for two-year-old Rosa, her head full of golden curls. My own bonnet is hot pink with tiny flowers.

This year, July 24 falls on a Sunday. I am up early, standing barefoot on the kitchen linoleum, my hands squeezing cream of chicken soup through frozen shredded potatoes. Two Pyrex casseroles of Jell-O are already cooling in the refrigerator, ready for our annual Pioneer Day dinner, an event that delights my curious non-Mormon friends and horrifies my sweet Jewish husband. David maintains his urbane culinary preferences like he was keeping kosher. To him, classic Mormon cuisine is totally *treif*, the bottom-feeding depths of *goyishe*: long-suffering Crock-Pot pot roast, Jell-O dishes with canned fruit and dairy product, white rolls, iceberg lettuce, and ranch dressing.

Right now I am making the hallmark Mormon dish: funeral potatoes, a heart-stopping, lipid-sodden, church-dinner comfort food—two 32-ounce bags of frozen shredded potatoes, two cans cream of chicken soup, two cups sour cream, a cup of grated cheese, a half cup butter, mixed together and topped with cornflakes, then baked in a 350-degree oven, serves twelve. As I stir the melted butter in with the potatoes, David sits at the kitchen table with the *New York Times*, shaking his head to perform his revulsion. Ella and Rosa dance about my ankles, unclad but for bonnets and cotton underpants. I harangue them about their pioneer ancestors: "Your great-great-great-grandmother crossed the plains when she was just your age. Would you be ready to do the same?"

My daughters are getting old enough now, Ella especially, to either grow or not to grow a living connection to Mormonism. And it has been—I count back—how many years since I have attended church myself? But I think of Ella and Rosa. How badly I want them to know what their grandmothers knew. How badly I want them to have a claim on the curious beauty and the power of this tradition. How badly I want them to make their own place in this Mormon world. My daughters embolden me with a renewed urgency to try again.

I rinse my hands and dance Ella and Rosa down the hallway to their bedroom. I kneel before them, slide pink dresses over their heads, and fasten the buckles on their sandals. I take off my hot-pink pioneer bonnet and zip myself into a dress. David, gamely, smiles and puts on a shirt and tie. We pack bags of snacks and games and snap the girls into their car seats. We arrive a few minutes late. I duck my head and move to the back of the chapel; David follows: we each have a girl by the hand. We set up a half circle of folding chairs in the overflow area. I position toy cars, dinosaurs, soft books, juice boxes, and Baggies of Cheerios. I herd Ella and Rosa while we all listen, more or less, to ritual retellings of the hardships of our pioneer ancestors. No one loves a tale of pioneer hardship better than I do. No one better loves the pioneer babies born in oxcarts and rude tents, rain pouring through the ceiling, sisters holding tin plates to collect water and shelter the mother in travail. No one better loves the frostbitten pioneer feet and toes, partially amputated with a butcher knife. No one better loves the old pioneer ladies inspired by the Holy Ghost to arrive on the doorstep at midnight with a medicinal poultice. No one—*no one*, I tell you—loves a good pioneer poultice more than I do.

After the last speaker the congregation sings the beloved hymn of our Mormon exodus to Zion:

*Come, come, ye Saints, no toil or labor fear;*
*But with joy, wend your way.*
*Though hard to you this journey may appear,*
*Grace shall be as your day.*

*We'll find the place which God for us prepared,*
*Far away in the West.*
*Where none shall come to hurt or make afraid*
*And the Saints will be blessed.*

Even when I had no idea where I was headed, or where I was to lead my daughters, every night, I have sung all four verses to my daughters Ella and Rosa in the rocking chair. Now four years old, Ella knows the words by heart. Hearing them rendered not just by my solo voice but by a congregation of hundreds is to her a revelation. She cocks her head, arrested. She leaps to the aisle, scattering dinosaurs and juice boxes. She explodes into interpretive dance. She spins.

She sails. She waves her arms. She shakes her hips and sings into her thumb as though it were a microphone. In some churches, liturgical dance is an honored art form. Ours is not one of them.

Oh, I am glad to see Ella do her irreverent dance, to see her bones recognize this music, to see her know the songs her ancestors sang. I am not the same kind of Mormon girl I was when I was seven, eight, or eighteen years old. I am not an orthodox Mormon woman like my mother. I am an unorthodox Mormon woman with a fierce and hungry faith. And I need Ella and Rosa to remember the words to the pioneer songs just like I need them to remember all that risks being forgotten in a Mormonism where telling unorthodox versions of our story is sometimes viewed as the work of enemies and apostates.

I am not an enemy, and I will not be disappeared from the faith of my ancestors. I am the descendant of Mormon pioneers. Sometimes, even in my own tradition, I feel a long way from home. But I will keep on crossing as many plains as this life puts in front of me. I drag along my Jewish husband, my two daughters, and a trunk of difficult questions. Through snow, sagebrush, and rattlesnakes, I reach the edge of the valley. I hunker beneath my wide-brimmed calico bonnet and wait for a sign. I look to my daughters. Ella does her joyful dance at the margins of the wagon train, a wild dance in the desert, a wild dance to bring the rain.

# 11

# protect marriage

Months after I decide to take my daughters back to church, the Mormon grapevine brings word that an announcement will be read from the pulpit on Sunday morning to congregations across California:

> *In March 2000 California voters overwhelmingly approved a state law providing that "Only marriage between a man and a woman is valid or recognized in California." The California Supreme Court recently reversed this vote of the people. On November 4, 2008, Californians will vote on a proposed amendment to the California state constitution that will now restore the March 2000 definition of marriage approved by the voters. . . . We ask that you do all you can to support the proposed constitutional amendment by donating*

> *of your means and time to assure that marriage in California is legally defined as being between a man and a woman. . . .*

I feel as if my heart has been thrown to the concrete and a cinder block dropped on it.

The same way I felt when my church declared feminists, intellectuals, and gays and lesbians its enemies in 1993.

My heart on the concrete, a cinder block on my heart.

That summer a vast and professionally orchestrated grassroots campaign grinds into action, mobilizing Mormon congregations. Mormons are asked to donate about eight hours a month to the Yes on 8 campaign, but especially in conservative Southern California, many Mormons volunteer to give two or three times more. They do so because heterosexual marriage holds a uniquely sacred place in Mormon theology: marriages performed in Mormon temples are a saving rite necessary to entering the highest levels of heaven. They do so because they fear that legalizing same-sex civil marriages will prove to endanger the Church's ability to perform its own temple marriages. And they do so, most important, because they have been asked, and they have promised, always to obey, give, and serve. Although I do not believe that same-sex civil marriages pose a legal threat to the religious freedom of the Church, I understand and acknowledge the powerful pull of duty Mormons all around me are feeling, for I have felt it too. As the old pioneer hymn urges:

*The world has need of willing men,*
*Who share the workers' zeal,*
*Come help the good work move along,*
*Put your shoulder to the wheel.*

Because Mormon congregations are usually organized by geographical districts that map very neatly onto voter precincts, the Church mobilizes with breathtaking speed and efficiency. Clipboards are circulated during Sunday meetings. Check the column: canvass, phone bank, data entry, child care. At the first statewide precinct walk on August 16, almost thirty thousand Yes on 8 volunteers fan out into neighborhoods, knocking on doors, identifying and recruiting likely voters to "protect marriage" by eliminating the civil marriage rights of gays and lesbians.

The man in charge of the vast Mormon Proposition 8 grassroots operation is Grant Jensen, my childhood bishop, the professional Republican pollster and strategist. Now Grant Jensen tells the world, "If same-sex marriage advocates win, the whole structure collapses: the family, the nation, and in time civilization itself." Brother Jensen has a gay son.

Meanwhile, in Northern California, a Mormon woman named Laura Compton starts Mormons for Marriage, a website and social network to support marriage equality and connect Mormons who feel that for reasons of conscience they cannot support the Church's Yes on 8 campaign. In 2000, when Mormons mobilized in support of California's

Defense of Marriage Amendment, a young gay Mormon man named Stuart Mathis killed himself on the steps of a California ward house. Laura Compton is the mother of two small children. Her goal: no more suicides this time.

In August, we learn that the Yes on 8 campaign has set fundraising goals for each Mormon congregation: higher goals are set for congregations in wealthy areas with higher monthly tithing receipts. Church leaders place donation forms in the foyers of Mormon ward houses to track how well congregations are meeting their contribution goals. Special phone calls are arranged between high-income California Mormons and high-ranking members of the Church leadership, who suggest that these families each donate $25,000 to the Yes on 8 campaign. Obedience follows. By the middle of August, dozens and dozens of $25,000 contributions begin to materialize on the California secretary of state's election donation reporting website. We see it all there: Mormon first names like Rulon, Spencer, Lynn, and Brigham; Mormon last names like Christianson, Allred, and Rigby. Our parents, our siblings, our Sunday School teachers, our piano teachers, the boys we once kissed in the church parking lot.

I stay home most Sundays during the Proposition 8 campaign. Too raw. Too much. Too soon. But in September, when my newborn nephew is named and blessed back home in Orange County, I return to the very ward where I was a little girl. Orange County is ground zero for the Mormon Yes on 8 campaign. Grant Jensen stands in the foyer and shakes hands all around. I sit in the pews with my sisters and watch as a circle of men in dark suits—my brother, my father, my brothers-in-law—take the baby in their arms to bless him. After the prayer, my brother holds beautiful baby Evan aloft in his little white and blue suit.

Words about protecting marriage find their way into every prayer and talk that day. I shift in my seat. I feel the grind of concrete against flesh against cinder block. I devise a reason to leave the chapel: my two-year-old daughter Rosa is fussy and needs to be walked.

Slowly, with Rosa in my arms or toddling down the hall in front of me, I circle the corridors of the church where I grew up. I see the cool-walled classrooms where I watched *Man's Search for Happiness*, with longing pulling through the center of my chest. I see the rooms where Sister Tucker and Sister Williams taught us first-aid skills for Girls Camp. I see the cultural hall where Natasha and I practiced our dance festival routine. Then I turn a corner, and I see it there, in the foyer: a red milk crate on a table.

I walk closer. Inside the red milk crate, I see sign-up sheets, canvass instruction sheets, and clipboards full of information on Yes on 8 voters identified during the canvass the day before. I have canvassed. I know how painstaking and time-expensive the work is, how precious this data, the hours and hours of door knocking it took to collect.

My heart pounds. I look around. The hallways are clear.

*It is not good to steal. It is not good to destroy the hard work of others. It is not good to be angry.*

My heart pounds. I take the sheets from the clipboard and shove them in my pink-flowered diaper bag. I pick up Rosa, put her on my hip, and walk quickly, nonchalantly, outside into the parking lot. My high heels click against the asphalt. Should I keep the canvassing sheets safely hidden in my pink-flowered diaper bag or get them off my person? I spy a metal grate in the sidewalk of the church parking lot. Shielded by a row of cars, Rosa still on my hip, I squat in my high heels and shove the canvassing sheets under the metal grate.

Still, I feel the weight of the cinder block on my heart on the ground.

In September, word comes that a million plastic yellow Yes on 8 lawn signs scheduled to materialize on lawns across the state as a crucial element in the grassroots Yes on 8 visibility campaign have been inexplicably delayed at the manufacturing plant in China. Long dreading the day when the Yes on 8 lawn signs popped up in my own neighborhood, I feel a sense of relief.

Meanwhile, at the local No on 8 headquarters, volunteers parsimoniously dole out a few American-made, union-made No on 8 signs. "Where do you live?" they ask, brows wrinkled. The real truth is that there is not yet enough money in the No on 8 campaign to give signs away to anyone who wants one.

I start putting in phone-banking shifts at the No on 8 headquarters in Hillcrest, San Diego's gay neighborhood. "I am a Mormon," I tell the room of volunteers whenever I am asked to introduce myself. I sit at a little table with Buddy and Tom, married five months. All three of us are wearing headsets plugged into laptop computers. The computer dials down old Democratic party lists. I read from a script. I talk to a few answering machines. Most of the numbers are bad. I read the names on my screen and imagine plumbers in Pacoima, schoolteachers in El Cajon. Someone in the next room gets an old man on the line shouting about Leviticus. He is an old man in a state where farmlands sit fallow for want of water, prisons have been built on farmlands, factories closed, and children of people who used to work in the factories have been sent to prisons. And old men shout about Leviticus. *Put your shoulder to the wheel.* Soon, the battery on my cell phone dies. There are extra laptop computers but no extra phones. I go to the bathroom and cry.

On Sundays during the Proposition 8 campaign, I sneak over to the great gray Episcopal cathedral across town. St. Paul's stands on a palm-tree-lined avenue at the edge of Balboa Park. About half of the parishioners are gay. It is cool inside the great gray cathedral. Married old men in elegant suits present themselves at the altar for communion. My girls sit with me in the pews and color on clipboards while I stare at a wooden Jesus on the cross suspended above the altar. It is an unfamiliar sight: this Jesus, arms outstretched and bound, on a cross, suspended in the chapel. Mormons do not have crucifixes in our chapels. I cry. By now my girls are used to my crying. Five-year-old Ella wrinkles her face and sticks her fingers in my wet eyes, curious, compassionate.

Camellias bloom red in the St. Paul's Cathedral courtyard. After services, I stop by a table for the No on 8 campaign. I sign up for another phone-bank shift. I tell them I am a Mormon. I always feel the need to tell them I am Mormon.

Hearing the word *Mormon*, the No on 8 tablers begin to chat vacantly, distantly, with bitterness.

"I know where a Mormon church building is," says one.

"I *am* a Mormon," I repeat myself, quietly. "That is why I am here."

Another No on 8 volunteer, a clear-eyed African-American woman, understands me.

"Oh," she says, nodding, returning my gaze. She understands what it means to be the only one in the room and why it matters.

By October, a few polls suggest that opponents of Proposition 8 have a small lead. The polls, I know, are wrong. Only a few newspapers have glimpsed the scale of the Mormon Yes on 8 campaign. All day, every day, I walk around in a daze, a head-to-toe state of alarm.

One October Sunday evening, the Church convenes a satellite broadcast to deliver instructions from headquarters in Salt Lake City on how to get out the vote on Election Day. Thousands of Mormons fill the pews in ward houses across California. It is the largest, most effective political volunteer training I have ever witnessed.

That same weekend, at a professional meeting, I see an old friend, a professor at the University of California who now spends most of his time in France. He is blond, handsome, political—an aging surfer boy with a copy of *Le Monde* tucked under his elbow.

"Sweetheart, what's wrong?" he asks, sensing my distress.

"Proposition 8," I tell him. "It's going to win. You know what my people are doing?"

He smiles affectionately and kisses me on the forehead.

"Poor thing," he says. "It's okay." Then, a pause, as if confidentially. "You know, there aren't that many of your people."

I stare at him blankly. I try not to think he is a fool.

I feel like I am coming down with a fever and go back to my hotel room, where for hours I pace the floor, then get on my knees and put my face down in the bed. I open a space in the middle of my chest and sob through it. If my prayer had words, they would sound like this: Dear God, I know you see all of this. I know you are on both sides of the story. Help me know what to do. Help me know how to feel. Soften everyone's hearts, including mine.

As the campaign grinds into its final weeks, phone banks are mobilized up and down the Mormon corridor, at ward houses in Idaho, at Brigham Young University. Mormons are hustled to the phone banks. Emails fly: "Satan is trying to shut down the temples in California." Across the United States, rank-and-file Mormons are being told that the legalization of civil gay marriage in California will require churches to sanctify gay marriages or else face massive penalties that will force them to close. They are being told that gay civil marriage rights threatens our freedom of belief and worship. Every newspaper, every legal analyst in the country has declared that this is a falsehood. But many believe. They obey. They fill phone banks. Rich Mormons across the country are hit up for huge last-minute donations: seven million dollars from individual donors in the last seventy-two hours of the campaign.

I start hearing from other Mormons that people have stolen their Yes on 8 signs, left dog feces on their front steps, and thrown bleach on peaceful Yes on 8 demonstrators. Thousands of Mormons line Pacific Coast Highway one night to demonstrate support for the proposition. The television cameras do not come.

Laura at Mormons for Marriage asks me to speak at a No

on 8 event in Redlands, deep within the Inland Empire, Yes on 8 territory. Others on the program include a legal expert, a Christian minister, and a rabbi. "Can anyone else do it?" I ask her. Laura tells me most of her other Southern California contacts are unavailable. She says she could fly down, but she would have to leave her kids. It would be a very fast trip, and very expensive. I agree to help.

The Church has said that it respects the rights of its members with dissenting opinions. Still, as I write my speech, terror sits on my chest. I wrestle with the specter of excommunication that haunts every dissenting Mormon who writes or speaks in public. I wrestle with silence. I carefully arrange my words on the paper, trying to describe the exact shape and weight of the cinder block I feel on my heart. I have not spoken about matters like this to my own family in many, many years.

Encouragement comes from my friend Soledad, who is gay. On Wednesday afternoon, she sees me at the school where our daughters attend kindergarten together. She looks at my face and takes pity. "It's time to come out of the closet," she says. She holds my hand.

On Thursday night, I click the mouse to send my speech to my parents, brother, sisters.

On Friday morning, I get an email from my father.

"We want you to know we love you," the email says. "You have wanted a more just and loving world since you were a little girl."

Tears drop on my keyboard. My chest heaves.

My husband, my girls, and I leave for Redlands early Saturday morning. When we arrive at the church, as the minister, the rabbi, the legal expert, and I meet to prepare for the event, I can hear old men calling up and yelling about Leviticus into the church's answering machine.

Among the crowd are many gay Mormons, including one of the paid staff for the No on 8 campaign. I recognize her blond hair, her clear and riveting blue eyes, her narrow features; I hear the remnant of a Mormon Utah accent rounding her speech. We embrace each other deeply. I can feel her ribs through her T-shirt. She tells me she is the niece of a prominent member of the church leadership. She once served an eighteen-month mission for the Church. She spent many years in deep depression, crying on her knees. When she finally came out of the closet, she tells me, she felt a burning in her bosom, an overwhelming feeling of peacefulness and love from her Heavenly Father. Her partner is here at the rally with her. Her family does not speak to her.

I give my speech, voice shaking. I ask the crowd to sign up for an election shift with the Mormon No on 8 organizers. I sing the crowd our old pioneer song:

*Put your shoulder to the wheel; push along,*
*Do your duty with a heart full of song.*
*We all have work; let no one shirk.*
*Put your shoulder to the wheel.*

After I finish, an old man stands at the back of the crowd, hollering about Leviticus and calling out each of us speakers with an angry pointed finger. "He's not a real rabbi," he screams at the rabbi. "You're not a real Mormon," he screams at me. One of the gay Mormons in the crowd, a broad-shouldered lesbian, quietly walks over and places her body between the screaming man and the crowd. The minister leads us in singing "This Little Light of Mine." The old man walks back to his pickup truck in the parking lot.

After the meeting, people confess with tears in their eyes how difficult it has been to bear the unthinking self-righteousness and cruelty of some of their Mormon coworkers and neighbors. They tell me that their No on 8 signs have been stolen from their front lawns, dog feces left on their doorsteps, and acid thrown on No on 8 demonstrators. The crowd at the church in Redlands is small. Television cameras do not come.

On the eve of the election, on Monday night, in Salt Lake City, Mormon mothers of gay children organize a candlelight vigil. "Stop saying mean things about our kids!" brave white-haired Millie Watts tells the television cameras.

Across the West, the Yes on 8 phone banks burn all night long, turning out the vote, while gay people and their allies line the streets and hold candles.

Candles is how we ask for mercy when we know very well what is to come.

It is not good to be angry. *Put your shoulder to the wheel.*

When it is all over, Proposition 8 passes by a margin of 52.3 percent to 47.7 percent.

It is the most expensive ballot initiative fight over a social issue in California history: eighty-two million dollars. Mormon individual donors account for at least 50 percent of the money raised in support of Proposition 8.

An oral rehydration packet for a child with diarrhea costs about 10 cents. Diarrhea is the second leading cause of death among children worldwide. Diarrhea kills five thousand children each day, almost two million children each year. Eighty-two million dollars buys almost one billion oral rehydration packets, enough to provide life-saving treatment for every child on the globe with diarrhea for a decade to come.

A few days after the election, outraged gays and lesbians and their allies rally by the tens of thousands at Mormon temples in San Diego and Los Angeles.

I do not attend the rallies. I read news coverage, and I laugh at some of the picket signs: "You have two wives, I want one!" Other signs are more ugly, angry, hurt: "Liars burn in hell." Would have been nice, I think, if you all would have been out in August and September, canvassing eight hours a month.

It is not good to be angry. *Put your shoulder to the wheel.*

The protesters do not understand that picketing at Mormon temples inflames a centuries-old persecution complex: deep memories of mobs amassing in Missouri, of temples abandoned and destroyed in Ohio and Illinois. More reason for Mormons to circle the wagons and to feel like an embattled righteous minority.

Women stand in a little cluster at my sister's ward house in Utah. "I never thought I would live to see the last days," one says, hanging her head, tearful. "I never knew it would look like this."

A few weeks after the election, Grant Jensen publishes a glossy coffee-table book: *How Americans View Mormonism*. The book is full of little colored bar charts and pie graphs, like the ones I used to print out at his office when I was fifteen. His findings? Forty-nine percent of Americans have unfavorable impressions of Mormons; 37 percent have favorable ones.

My dad relays even more specific elements of Brother Jensen's findings to me: in our Orange County, he relates, surveys show more people would rather vote for a Muslim than a Mormon. His chest is tight with surprise, a knot in his throat. He recedes a bit against the world he inhabits.

I look up Grant Jensen's son Mark. I haven't seen him since we were both children in the same Orange County congregation. We reconnect by email. *How are you?* I ask. *Okay*, he says. He is living with his boyfriend in San Bernardino. He recounts the day he stumbled upon stacks of Proposition 8 campaign materials in his father's office and realized the magnitude of what was to come. He and his parents haven't spoken since.

Three months after the election, I bring myself and my daughters back to church. I generally opt out of the adult meetings, preferring instead to sit in the back of my daughters' primary classes, where the talk is about God and Jesus and prayer and pioneers and not about the adult business of protecting marriage.

Eventually, though, I do venture back into Relief Society. The teacher, a dark-haired woman in her fifties, has outlined on the chalkboard the lesson plan straight from the Salt Lake City–issued manual. But her talk keeps veering sharply away from the lesson plan, to the strain of Proposition 8, flak taken by Mormon high school students during the Yes on 8 campaign, the anti-Mormon sentiment of the television show *Big Love*, Tom Hanks's recent talk show declaration that Mormons are "un-American," and a searching postelection feature on the Church in the pages of *Time* magazine.

The campaign has taken a toll on every one of us.

I try to distract myself by checking my text messages, then I start keeping score. Fifteen minutes into the lesson:

stories relating to Proposition 8 or anti-Mormon sentiment resulting from Proposition 8, 5; stories relating to Jesus, 0.

The air is heavy with defensiveness, and *man*, how I miss Jesus. I consider getting up and leaving the room just to spare myself the frustration. I think about sitting in my car and having a cry. But I don't. I hold my tongue, but I also hold my seat. This is a church inhabited by people willing to give up their own children for being gay. This is also the church of Millie Watts and the church of my grandmothers. This is a church of tenderness and arrogance, of sparkling differences and human failings. There is no unmixing the two.

There is no way around Proposition 8: being a Mormon in California will mean dealing with its legacy of hard feelings, in our families, in our churches, in our neighborhoods, for years and years to come. Yes, like it or not, by putting ourselves front and center in the battle against gay civil rights, we Mormons have married ourselves to gay folks for a long, long time.

I consummate my own personal relationship to the marriage equality movement in March when I attend Camp Courage, a weekend-long event where they train activists to tell our own stories about why equality matters and to use our stories as we phone bank and canvass, to change the political landscape of California, one conversation at a time. This is the same door-to-door, face-to-face grassroots strategy used by the Obama presidential campaign. *Put your shoulder to the wheel!*

At Camp Courage San Diego, I see a few familiar faces from the No on 8 campaign—Buddy and Tom from the phone bank, and Richard, a tall slender gay man in his late sixties wearing round Michel Foucault–style glasses and an *Angels in America* T-shirt. Richard has been married to his husband Tom for thirty-one years.

I tell him that I am Mormon.

"Brigham Young University did things to our people," Richard tells me, his face long and pale, but without blame. "Electroshock therapy. If they found out you were gay, they'd threaten to tell your family, kick you out of school and the church unless you did the electroshock aversion therapy."

Yes, I nod. I know.

To begin the training, Camp Courage attendees gather in small groups where, under the guidance of Obama campaign veterans, we scribble the elements of our personal stories on preprinted handouts.

My page fills quickly. The other folks in the group notice. "Look at the star student over there," a pretty brown-haired woman kindly teases me.

After we write, we tell our stories to one another. Everyone in the circle has a story worth telling: stories of being disowned by families and beaten up by classmates, stories of running away and starting over, stories of consciously choosing a life of dignity and fulfillment. But I am the only Mormon girl. To them, my story is a revelation. When the Camp Courage organizers call on each group to choose one member to tell her story to the entire camp, my group pushes me forward.

Lisa, the woman leading Camp Courage, puts her arm around my shoulders and brings me up to the stage. "Now, this is Joanna," she tells the crowd, with a giant smile. "And we are gonna show her the love." Two hundred gay rights activists come to their feet.

"My name is Joanna," I say. "And I am a straight Mormon feminist."

(The crowd cheers.)

"I grew up in the orange groves of Republican Orange County. I was raised to believe in a loving, kind, and powerful God—"

(A voice comes from the front row—"Yes!" Someone is testifying along.)

"In 1993, one of the leaders of my church declared feminists, intellectuals, and gays and lesbians enemies.

"I felt as if someone had thrown my heart to the concrete and dropped a cinder block on it.

"In 1997, my church started giving hundreds of thousands of dollars to antigay marriage initiatives.

"I felt as if someone had thrown my heart to the concrete and dropped a cinder block on it.

"For years afterward, I cried almost every time I set foot in a Mormon church."

(A wave of tenderness.)

"But I went back to church so that my daughters could know the same loving, kind, and powerful God I was raised to believe in.

"Just a few months later, my Church mobilized a huge campaign for Proposition 8.

"And again I felt as if someone had thrown my heart to the concrete and dropped a cinder block on it.

"I did what I could. It wasn't enough. But I am a Mormon. And I am not giving up."

No one boos. No one makes me feel ashamed. Everyone shows Mormon girl the love.

*Courage.*

I tell my story. The cinder block lifts, and my heart comes up off the ground.

# 12

# gathering the tribes

"What if one woman told the truth about her life?" mused the poet Muriel Rukeyser. "The world would split apart."

Sometimes the world does split apart, but writing can help put it back together.

I first started writing about faith when I was seven years old, and I published a poem about the baby Jesus in a Mormon children's magazine. For a long season in the middle of my life, I quit trying to organize experience into words. It was too hard and too painful. But not long after my second daughter was born, words came back to me again. I realized that my language was furnishing the world Ella and Rosa lived in. Ella turned two and started to attend a Jewish preschool, her modest vocabulary expanding to include words like *Shabbat*, *seder*, and *mitzvah*. It was up to me to give her a few Mormon words as well—*ward, sacrament, pioneer.* More important, it was up to me and David to develop a verbal architecture that would shelter the interfaith shape of her small life. Every night after the girls' bedtime, at a wobbly, makeshift desk pressed up against the edge of the front room in our nine-hundred-square-foot rental in San Diego, I came back to writing. I wrote at first about what was closest to me: my own interfaith family. My Jewish husband, our two Mormon-Jewish daughters, our little gathered tribe and the small world we were making together. My fingers made questions, prayers, and confessions.

Soon there was a manuscript, then an agent, then a New York City editor on the phone. "You're a terrific writer," she said, as I pressed my ear to the receiver. "There are so many interfaith families hungry to read this kind of book. There's just one thing . . ."

Her voice broke off. She paused.

"It's just too *Mormon.* I'm afraid people will find it a little *weird.* It wouldn't be a problem if you were, like, Presbyterian or something."

And so, ornery soul that I am, I went back to my writing desk, and every night after the girls' bedtime, I began to write down all the Mormon stories, ancestral tales handed down by my grandmother, lessons patiently taught by my parents at the kitchen table, memories from my own Mormon youth.

As I wrote my stories, I repopulated my world with all of the people who made me: Sister Pierce with her strawberry pie, Natasha and all the girls I danced with in the Rose Bowl, all the Girls Camp leaders, all the suit-wearing men sitting in swivel chairs behind formica-top desks, my Brigham Young University professors, and my Mormon feminist heroes too. All of them. Together. In my stories. As I wrote, I brought myself back from my own exile, the silent excommunication I subjected myself to when I was convinced Mormonism was not safe for women like me. I started to look up old friends, ones I'd lost during my exile years. I started to reconnect with the liberal Mormon kids with whom I'd shared college. "Where have you been?" they asked. "We missed you. Welcome back."

Just as Sister Simmons once strung together burnt umber and brassy yellow acrylic yarn as an offering of herself to the community, I strung together words. In those nouns and verbs and adjectives, I knit back together the parts of me that were never supposed to fit: Faithful. Unorthodox. Feminist. Mormon. It was from all the Mormon stories I heard growing up that I learned that salvation meant belonging. In writing my story, I found that salvation happens not only when our people claim us, but when we muster up the courage and the capacity to claim our own people—including the ones who have been pushed or left out.

As I wrote, I started to put small bits of prose out on the internet: some personal stories, and some essays probing important and conflicted parts of Mormon experience. The mail came quickly, some of it like rocks against the side of the house. Stinging words from strangers calling me a "wolf in sheep's clothing," an "anti-Mormon," an "apostate," a "liar." They told me I would be excommunicated for voicing such unorthodox sentiments. They accused me of not knowing the faith, of perverting the faith, of seeking to harm other Mormons by writing candidly about the tender places in Mormon life, the sparkling differences and human failings of our people.

Late one night, with the girls asleep, I read through an especially harsh batch of email from strangers. I left the house to run a late-night errand and found myself numb behind the steering wheel, my heart pounding, adrenaline running across my chest and down my arms. I remembered the shame I felt that February day decades ago at Brigham Young University when strangers in a passing car had called me an "anti-Christ" for pinning my peace-sign button to my book bag. What to do with these feelings? What to do with what felt like meanness from my own people? I scrutinized myself intensely: What if they were right? What if people like me were unworthy to tell our version of the Mormon story?

What if our voices did not deserve a place in the community? I felt a baffling sadness begin to seep back in. I parked my car under a streetlamp in the Target parking lot. Sitting behind the steering wheel, I did what my Mormon teachers had taught me to do whenever I was hurt or in danger. I did what I had done during the most difficult moments of the exile years: I prayed. I prayed to a God who stood beyond the human struggles and squabbles of day-to-day Mormonism. I prayed to the God my visiting teacher Sister Bryson told me would help me no matter what because I was searching for truth. I squeezed my eyes shut, and I opened my chest to God. *What should I do with the castigation and the shame? Are these voices speaking the words you want me to hear?* That's when I realized that through all the years of searching, from the time I was a small girl kneeling at the bedside on her orange prayer rug, I had learned what the voice of God sounded like. I knew what the voice of God felt like, and it did not feel like rocks against the side of the house. It did not leave a sting of shame burning across my temples and in the pit of my stomach. The voice of the God I knew was gentle, kind, and deliberate. And that voice was not forbidding me to write or speak, as long as I did so honestly and without malice. Even if I made mistakes from time to time, as a writer or as a Mormon, that voice would not condemn me. It would guide me firmly and gently through.

• • •

In time, another kind of mail began to reach my in-box, from other Mormons:

> "Thank you for saying things I want to say but don't know how."
>
> "I feel so relieved to think I can be myself at church."
>
> "I am a believing Mormon woman, and I'm worried that the church seems to be losing so many women."
>
> "I've always questioned, and I've always felt so alone. I don't feel alone any more."
>
> "I can have doubts without being forced to leave my faith behind. I don't know who I am if I am not Mormon."
>
> "I am gay, but I never stopped believing in the values I learned at church. Thank you for giving some voice to what I have felt."
>
> "I have always felt the way you described but never had the words to articulate it."

I am not special. I am just someone who happens to have the words. And this is how I would like to use them.

As I wrote, I met dozens of young women, some with pierced noses and spiky haircuts, pregnant, their shoulders curled, young husbands in tow, everyone crying, saying thank you, and me crying and saying thank you too. I met women with long, just-washed hair, no makeup, and babies on their hips who said, "The Spirit spoke to me today, and I felt impressed to drive across town and tell you to keep going." Older Mormon feminists reached out to put a steadying hand on my back or a soothing hand on my forehead. A thousand new Mormon friends materialized from out of thin air, each one nodding, strapping on his or her boots, picking up their piece of the handcart, saying, "Yes, let's walk together."

As I wrote, agnostic Catholics, reform Jews, gay Christian girls, even stone-cold atheists, gave me a hard look, then nodded, and said: "Yes, I recognize something familiar in the story you are telling."

As I wrote, the sun came up in the east and moved across the sky until it stood over my house among the remnant orange trees in San Diego. As I wrote, I found myself sitting more comfortably in the Sunday pew. As I wrote, my prayers changed from "God, please help me," to "God, thank you, and let me be useful."

And the more I learned to tell my own unorthodox story in public, the more I have learned how to tell the unorthodox story of my Mormon faith. Without shame, without hiding, without apologizing for it or myself, I have written about the misunderstandings that follow this young American faith, its human history, its awkwardness, its inventiveness, and its growing pains—all of them on record and plainly visible in the light of modern times.

These days, it's still acceptable to make fun of Mormons in public, to ridicule our history on television, to mock rituals we hold sacred, and to talk about us as though we are not in the room. Mormons have lived with such talk for centuries now, and over the years we have acquired an entire set of habits to cope. In the nineteenth century, faced with outsider hostility and ridicule, we gathered into our own settlements, created Zion communities in a string of midwestern towns, left behind our dearly bought temples each time we removed farther westward, and soon enough left behind the United States altogether to settle in Utah territory. When the federal government sent armies to war against Utah Mormons in the 1850s and 1860s, or spies to pursue and punish polygamists in the 1880s and 1890s, we learned to keep our stories to ourselves. We grew guarded against outsiders, and sometimes we punished Mormons in our midst who asked questions or told an unapproved version of the Mormon story, as if they might betray and weaken us. Those habits have stayed with us all these years. For the most part, we are still an insular people, protective of our differences, guarded and anxious, and ready to walk away.

There is no way forward, I believe, but to tell our whole story. Not the made-for-television version, but the entire very imperfect story, the one that reveals the human flaws of the ones who came before us. The one that presents Mormons as a people who are earnest and industrious *and* satisfied sometimes with easy contradictions, sweetly tender *and* capable of ignorance and arrogance. A people of sparkling differences and human failings. A people chosen because we have chosen to be ourselves. A people who are not afraid to tell an unorthodox story full of angels, sacred groves, ancestor pioneers, sacrifice, and longing, because an unorthodox story is what history has given us to tell.

An unorthodox story is nothing to be ashamed of. It is something that deserves to be shared.

There are much worse things than telling an unorthodox story, much worse things than explaining oneself to strangers. I always hoped that I would never have to explain myself. From the time I was a teenager standing in the parking lot of the Rose Bowl dance festival counting buses, I thrilled to be in crowds of Mormons and dreamed of finding a Mormon husband with whom I could wordlessly share my faith, everything already understood.

But my story went another way. When an orthodox Mormon world seemed too difficult and dangerous a place for me, I traveled into the world outside and found myself Mormon still. So Mormon, in fact, that whenever I introduced myself, I found that the subject came up within just a few minutes. I'd sit back and register the reaction: the speechless pause, the look of surprise, mild shock, or even delight, from non-Mormon strangers and acquaintances. In my mind, I'd run through the host of associations the word *Mormon* immediately conjured up for them—polygamy, racism, archconservatism, secretiveness—then I'd see just how many of these preconceptions I could casually disappoint. At times I have encountered silliness and misunderstanding and even a spot of meanness. Nothing to compare to the kind of meanness I experienced from born-again Christians when I was a teenager, or to what I'd experienced from other Mormons who suspected my unorthodox kind. No, what I found most of all was either polite reticence or a humane curiosity, and in the gracious space it afforded, a safe haven where I could tell my stories for the first time. Sharing humanized us all, both the Mormons in the stories and the non-Mormons who had feared, judged, or misunderstood us.

It was to this sweet space of talking, listening, and learning that I committed myself for life when I married David, a man whose religious practice entails a combination of Judaism, Buddhism, and ESPN. For fifteen years now, we have tried to understand each other, motivated by a sense of curiosity, rooted in respect and humor, and, going even deeper than that, a bedrock of loyalty. We will walk this life together. It has never been entirely easy but neither has it been impossibly difficult. There have been awkward and tearful moments. Our families have worried out loud and in private. Religious leaders have wrinkled their brows. The interfaith family guidebooks have counseled David and me to choose one tradition in which to raise the children, lest we confuse them, or water down both traditions so that we give them nothing at all—nothing but a watered-down and vaguely God-scented gruel.

But being the cantankerous souls that we are, David and I have smiled and largely ignored them. He is Jewish and I am Mormon, and to put away either one of our stories, our families, our peoples, to hold back these huge parts of ourselves from our children seems more damaging than the confusion that well-meaning people grimly prognosticate. Every family story has a great question at its center, and we certainly have ours: What becomes of our children if they are not our spiritual apprentices, if we do not expect them to turn out exactly like us? What will happen if we educate them in both traditions, teach them to be responsible to both traditions, and then expect them to make their own adult faith choices, as all grown-up children must someday do?

So here we are, a Jewish father and a Mormon mother, with Mormon-Jewish children, living a great experiment, aware that we may be failures—and yet each of us, busily, joyfully, trying to explain as much as we can to each other, competing for oxygen every night around the kitchen table. Each of us knows how to pray in at least two languages. We have worked to master the customs of each other's day-to-day religious lives. David struggles with the homely everyday tasks of Mormon congregations, trying to remember how exactly to collapse the metal folding chairs ubiquitous to our ward houses. He politely smiles as well-meaning LDS people pepper him with detailed questions about Old Testament rituals, as if he himself—a kid raised Reform in Southern California—knew exactly what the Levites in the temples did with the burnt offerings. He stifles his sneezing and itching whenever the subject of Jesus arises, because he, like most Jewish people, has inherited something of a Jesus allergy, developed collectively over the last two thousand years.

For my part, I have learned to cook *latkes*, *kugel*, brisket, and *matzah brei*. I have taught myself all the holidays and their stories and learned to make dairy lunches for summer school at the conservative synagogue. I have sobbed my way through Kol Nidre, trying to take refuge behind big dark sunglasses, a Mormon feminist, who felt in so many ways a failure in her own faith, finding in the Yom Kippur prayer for release from broken promises the most reasonable words to describe my situation. I have largely given up Christmas—there is no tree in our house, no stockings at the hearth, and Santa Claus has never visited—out of a desire to make our home right for my Jewish husband and children. I have taught myself the *shema*, and then I taught it to my children: the Lord is our God, the Lord is One. Even if we reach for that God in two different languages, a mother and a father tongue.

Our daughters, Rosa and Ella, hear the great stories every

day: Eve tasting that world-shifting fruit of knowledge, Lehi leading his family toward the tree of life, Moses kneeling barefoot before the burning bush, Joseph Smith kneeling in a grove of trees with a heart full of questions. Esther standing regal and unafraid and claiming her own story. Slaves leaving Egypt, and pioneers crossing the plains. Confused though they may be, at least they'll have great material to work from.

When things get strained, we have learned to shrug our shoulders, laugh, and wait a little. Faith, after all, means knowing that the answers will come, in time. And some Sunday afternoons, when the work of our various institutional indoctrinations is done, we take the kids and the dog (who is sort of a pagan Episcopalian—that's another story) and walk the beach together.

As Rosa and Ella write their names in the sand and outrun the waves, David moves his hands and talks anxiously about professional basketball.

And I'll confess whether or not it has been one of those weeks when I've worried vaguely about my own excommunication. I don't know a progressive Mormon woman who doesn't worry about that from time to time, given the excommunications we witnessed in the 1990s.

"I've been running the tapes of my church court again," I tell David, half-joking, half-serious. It feels better to say it out loud than to hold it inside, the fear, whether founded or unfounded. I meditate on what it would mean to have my name scrubbed from the records of the church, removed from the files stored in the granite canyons east of Salt Lake City, severed from the names of my grandmother, my great-grandmothers, my ancestors. I remember the stories I have heard from other women who have been excommunicated: the anger and sadness that kept them crying for days and days. I wonder why any religion would care to do this to its own people.

As we walk, I review in my mind everything I have written for the last seven days, searching for the hazy spots where probity bleeds into conceit or meanness. That, I tell myself, is where the real danger lies.

"It's okay," I tell him. "I don't think it will happen this week."

"Oh, yeah?" he asks. He smiles, reassuringly.

The people I attend church with every Sunday, the people who teach my children their Book of Mormon stories—these people have never said an unkind word, never made me or my children feel ashamed. Still, I know that in times past, high-ranking Church leaders have asked local leaders to investigate women like me. I believe the Church is slowly outgrowing old habits of punishing the unorthodox. I believe, but this I do not know for sure. All I can do is place my trust in a faith stronger than fear. All I can do is tell my story and hope that it fosters mercy.

David knows. He has heard this all before, and he will patiently outwait it.

Sometimes he has stronger faith than I do.

Good thing I married him.

There's a pioneer hymn I first learned while sitting in the wooden pews at church: I still sing it at church, and I have on my iPod a grinding, plaintive rock-and-roll version sung by the Saber Rattlers, a band led by a bearded Mormon kid in New York City:

*Now, let us rejoice in the day of salvation*
*No longer as strangers on earth need we roam.*
*Good tidings are sounding to us and each nation*
*And shortly the hour of redemption will come.*

*We'll love one another and never dissemble*
*But cease to do evil and ever be one*
*And when the ungodly are fearing and tremble*
*We'll watch for the day when redemption will come.*

I used to dream that Zion was a place full of people just like me. It was a place where we all knew and followed the same rules, nodding along to the tunes of hymns we had long ago memorized. And I dreamed that I would arrive there with a station wagon full of perfectly pressed and groomed kids, a custom Marie Osmond haircut, a suit-wearing husband, and the names of my ancestors neatly organized in blue binders.

My vision is a bit less tidy now. There are all kinds of people passing through, from the farm-boy Mormon missionaries we have over for dinner now and then, to Buddhist monks in saffron robes I meet in front of the dairy case at the grocery store, from gay Navajo Mormons I encounter on the internet to the moms at the Jewish preschool. *No longer as strangers on earth need we roam.* Zion is not so much a place on the map as a longing for a place where all who really hunger for truth and goodness—and I mean *everyone*—can gather and finally rest. I feel that longing; oh, do I feel it. I feel it all the time.

On Sundays, when I was growing up, we were not allowed to watch television, except for the epic four-hour Cecil B. DeMille film *The Ten Commandments.* We'd sit in front of the television in our Sunday clothes, my sisters and brother and I, and we'd watch it all unfurl across the television screen, from baby Moses set on the river through the plagues and the exodus to the golden calf and the Promised Land. No scene was more thrilling to me than the moment when all the tribes of Israel gathered on the promenade of sphinxes that stood before Pharoah's city, and a strapping stonecutter Joshua (played by the unforgettable John Derek) and all of his fellow heralds sounded their *shofar*s and proclaimed the *shema*, and Moses (played by the incomparable Charlton Heston) raised his staff and the great movement from slavery to freedom commenced. How my heart thrilled when the exodus rolled across our television screen—the young, whip-scarred Hebrew families, and the Ethiopian bondsmen, and the old women clinging to the back of mules, and even some god-fearing Egyptians, and the children who got lost in the confusion of the crowd were swept up and onto the shoulders of strong men wearing Levite robes. *Yes*, I knew, we would all get there someday. Every last one of us.

Now, every spring, my daughters and I break out our DVD copy of *The Ten Commandments* for the Easter-Passover season. I sit on the couch with freckle-faced Ella and curly-haired Rosa, snuggled up under a quilt Mormon friends tied for me decades ago, just before I went away to Brigham Young University. We have snuggled together when I read them stories from the Book of Mormon, and we have snuggled together when I taught them the *shema*. Somehow, this feels just as significant.

"You see that? That big messy spiral of people, moving, trying to find God?" I ask them, as the exodus unfolds once again on screen.

"That right there is Zion. Get there however you can."

# 13

# the book of mormon girl

What do we do with ourselves when we find we have failed to become the adults we dreamed of as pious children?

What do we do when the church of our childhoods no longer treasures our names?

How do we react when we discover at the core of faith a knot of contradictions?

Do we throw it all out? Throw out all the strange and beautiful stories of angels at the bedside, holy books buried in the American hillsides, and seagulls swooping down from the Utah skies to eat up plagues of crickets?

Do we sue to get our tithes and offerings back, all the dollars we faithfully mailed to Salt Lake City, to build temples we would never see?

Do we blame our parents? Do we resent the worry in their

eyes? Do we feel our failures eat up the oxygen in the room like lost and hungry ancestors?

Do we blame the orthodox, so beautiful in their temple clothes, always doing as they are told, but so alone with their own forms of failure and sorrow?

Do we blame ourselves, for our treasonous prayers, for the fact that we took it all too seriously: all the talk of love, compassion, equality, mercy, and justice?

I don't want to blame anyone. I want to do what my ancestors did: look west and dream up a new country for my children. I just want to tell my story. Because the tradition is young, and the next chapter is yet to be written. And ours may yet be a faith that is big enough for all of our stories.

I want a faith as expansive as the skies above the Eastern Sierras at eleven thousand feet. I want to rest my back against lodgepole pines with you and puzzle out the mysteries. I want a faith as handmade as pioneer-carved wooden pews under an arching tabernacle sky dome. I want a faith as welcoming as a Pioneer Day dinner table set with a thousand cream-of-chicken-soup casseroles and wedding-present Crock-Pots, a table with room enough for everyone: male and female, black and white, gay and straight, perfect and imperfect, orthodox or unorthodox, Mormon, Jew, or gentile.

I want room at the table for all the gay and lesbian Mormons who feel they can't go home for dinner, and room for all the Mormon parents who don't know how to let them in the door.

Room for my Jewish husband, and all the non-Mormon people who patiently watch Mormon loved ones wrestle with our angels.

A place for my father, who taught me to read the Book of Mormon, and gently led me by the hand into the baptismal font.

And a place for my brother, who in his own way is teaching his sons to read the Book of Mormon, and gently leads them into the baptismal font.

Room for all the Idaho farm boys on their missions, lonely for video games.

All the men in their Sunday socks walking colicky babies across cold kitchen floors.

All the Mormon men who never dreamed of being prophets, never dreamed of taking plural wives, and even for those who did, at this table, there is room for you.

I want room for all the Mormon girls.

For all the Mormon pioneer girls, asafetida bags around their necks and rolling hoops between the Utah cottonwoods.

For all the Mormon girls living in Arizona suburbs with their minivans and mommy blogs and closets full of potato pearls sealed up against the end-times.

For all the Mormon girls keeping faith in the concrete canyons of New York City.

For Marie Osmond in all of her glorious variations: chubby thirteen-year-old Marie, perfect skinny college sophomore Marie, postpartum depression Marie, grown Marie *and* her grown lesbian daughter.

For Janice Allred, Margaret Toscano, Gail Houston, Cecilia Konchar Farr, Lavina Fielding Anderson, and all the other Mormon feminists, and for all the Mormon feminists who came before us, even Sonia Johnson, wherever she may be.

For Millie Watts, white-haired Mormon mother of a gay son, holding a candle in protest on a November evening.

For my mother, the genealogist who has rescued from oblivion the names of all our dead.

For my great-great-grandmother Martha Clayton who threatened to cut off her husband's ears if he took a plural wife, and for my great-great-great-grandmother Lucy Evalina Waterbury Wight who was a plural wife.

For the eighty-three-year-old Mormon woman patiently typing out her life story on a quiet springtime afternoon in a red-rock southern Utah town.

For the forty-year-old Mormon single mother hoping her car will start on a cold Wyoming morning.

For all the Mormon women with puffy hands and wide hips who have taught me how to camp under the stars, or filled my refrigerator with casseroles when I had my babies.

For all the Mormon girls shivering in basement apartments in Provo cutting oil paints with dull blades.

For all the tall skinny blond Mormon girls playing basketball in reservation border towns, and for all the Navajo Mormon girl point guards hungry to defeat them.

For all the Tongan Mormon girls, Guatemalan Mormon girls, Korean Mormon girls—the future belongs to you.

And for all the redheaded polygamous girls who boldly face the television cameras and say, "Don't feel sorry for us."

For my beautiful brown-haired sister who lives on the very face of the Wasatch Mountains, dreams of surfing, and bumps hip-hop from her minivan up and down the granite-walled canyons.

For my beautiful blond sister talking fast in the corporate boardroom and wearing her faith quietly against her skin.

For my Mormon-Jewish daughters, their faces a galaxy of freckles, standing in the sunlight in their soccer cleats.

For my beloved grandmothers standing right above them, dressed in white.

They all belong in my unorthodox Mormon story.

As do you: Catholic girl, Jewish girl, gay Christian, Baptist boy many miles away from home, grown man on a journey, grown woman not afraid.

May this story keep you company as you travel.

May it help nurture your own.

# acknowledgments

No one ever asks to have a writer in the family, or the ward. To all the people who find themselves in these pages, especially my parents, thank you for giving life its richness. Mom and Dad—I love you. Thank you for teaching me to love this faith and for your grace and patience.

The first draft of this manuscript was completed during a residency at Hedgebrook Women Writers in Residence on Whidbey Island, Washington. To learn more about how Hedgebrook supports Women Authoring Change, please visit hedgebrook.org.

I thank all of the communities of faith that have sheltered me—Congregation Dor Hadash of San Diego; the Friends Meeting of Austin, Texas; St. Paul's Cathedral of San Diego—and to thousands upon thousands of Mormons who have inspired me, taught me, frustrated me, challenged me, and delighted me in the many stakes of Zion.

I learned to write from Darrell Spencer, Louise Plummer, Leslie Norris, and Susan Howe at Brigham Young University and from David Wong Louie, Stephen Yenser, and Paula Gunn Allen at UCLA. Blessed encouragement has come from Lisa Moore, Jim Lee, Garnette Cadogan, Holly Welker, Carol Lynn Pearson, John Dehlin, Anne Peffer, Ann Davis, Tresa Edmunds, Cathy Castillo, Susan Scott, Sara Burlingame, Lisa Butterworth, Kristine Haglund, Steve Gibson, Susan Reed, Jana Riess, Claire Tichi Grezmekovsky, Trent Ricks, Phil Barlow, Mary Valle, Karen Maezen Miller, Sarah Posner, Lisa Webster, Evan Derkacz, the women with whom I shared the Hedgebrook farmhouse table, and many, many others.

David Kamper gave me heart. Every day.

Thank you to the women who had faith in this book and undauntedly made it happen: Jessica Ravitz, Rhoda Janzen, Claudia Cross at Folio, and Leah Miller and Jill Siegel at the Free Press. Matt Page crafted the original cover design.

Many names in this memoir have been anonymized to protect individuals' privacy, and a few story elements resequenced in the service of narrative.

In chapter 3, cited song lyrics are from Lex de Azevedo, "Saturday's Warrior," *Saturday's Warrior: Original Cast and Soundtrack*, Embryo Records, 1974. All references in chapter 4 are to Marie Osmond, *Marie Osmond's Guide to Beauty, Health & Style*, Touchstone Books, 1980; lyrics are from Julie de Azevedo, "Window to His Love," *Window to His Love*, Lumen, 2003. In chapter 5, cited song lyrics are from Evan

Stephens, "True to the Faith," *Hymns of the Church of Jesus Christ of Latter-day Saints*, published in Salt Lake City by the Church of Jesus Christ of Latter-day Saints, 1985.

An earlier version of chapter 3 appeared in the *Michigan Quarterly Review*.

# about the author

**Joanna Brooks** is a national voice on Mormon life and politics, an award-winning scholar of religion and American culture, and the author or editor of five books. She has been featured on American Public Media's *On Being,* NPR's *All Things Considered,* NPR's *Talk of the Nation,* BBC's *Americana, Interfaith Voices,* and *Radio West* and in the *New York Times,* the *Washington Post,* the *CNN Belief Blog,* and the *Huffington Post.* She is a senior correspondent for the online magazine *ReligionDispatches.org* and offers answers to seekers of all stripes at her own site askmormongirl.com. Follow @askmormongirl on Twitter or visit her at joannabrooks.org.

# the book of
# mormon girl

a memoir of an american faith

joanna brooks

## Reading Group Guide

## TOPICS AND QUESTIONS FOR DISCUSSION

1. What did you learn about Mormonism from this book? What assumptions or stereotypes about Mormons did you have before reading? How did this book cause you to reflect on your assumptions? What surprised you? What new insights did you gain? What questions do you now have about the faith?

2. Joanna describes how as a young girl, her religion's rules made her feel special, like "a root beer among the Coca-Colas." Were there things in your childhood that separated you from your peers? How did it feel to be different? Did you enjoy the feeling of being unique?

3. Marie Osmond was an important figure in Joanna's childhood because she was one of the very few celebrities from a similar background. Who were your celebrity role models growing up, and why?

4. When you were a child, how did you think about faith? How have your ideas or beliefs changed over time? Do you have a faith or spiritual practice now? How does it guide you?

5. When young Mormon men turn twelve years old, they are ordained into the lower ranks of the Latter-day

Saints (or, LDS) Church's lay priesthood. There is no comparable religious coming-of-age ceremony for young Mormon women, and Joanna remembers that when she got her first period—another coming-of-age moment—her grandmother told her it was a "curse." What coming-of-age rituals mark the entrance of girls into adulthood in American culture? Does your religion or culture have customs that honor this transition? How do coming-of-age rituals shape the way young women view themselves?

6. In the chapter on object lessons, Joanna describes sitting in a classroom with other young women and passing a rose around the room for each member of the circle to handle. At the end, when the rose is ruined after being handled by so many people, the young women are told that the rose was like their virtue; nobody would ever want that used flower. What kind of lessons did you hear about sexuality growing up? If you could, what would you say to your sixteen-year-old selves about sex?

7. In 1993, six members of the LDS Church were excommunicated. They were feminists and intellectuals who had written or spoken about controversial subjects. After this action by the Church, Joanna stepped away from the Mormon community for several years. Why do you think she took this step? Have you ever been in a sit-

uation where something you believed in took an action you disagreed with? How did you respond?

8. Joanna relates that she did not share most of her internal turmoil about her faith with her parents. She writes, "Perhaps I wanted to protect them from shame. Perhaps I wanted to protect myself from feeling the brunt of their shame." Are there elements of your life you were not or still are not able to share with your parents? Why?

9. Did your religion play a role in your selection of spouse? Did you marry within your faith? Outside your faith? How has your marriage shaped your relationship to your religion?

10. At several different points in her story, Joanna describes acts of kindness and understanding by friends, acquaintances, and strangers who made a difference to her as she struggled to find her way. Who stood out to you in the story as a mentor or guide? Who do you turn to in your life when you need spiritual advice?

11. The stories of her Mormon pioneer grandmothers give Joanna strength and inspiration for her journey, especially in the Pioneer Day chapter when she returns to church. Do you know your family history? Have you

traced your genealogy? What kinds of family stories do you draw inspiration from?

12. At the height of the Proposition 8 campaign, Joanna destroyed some campaign materials she found inside the Mormon church building where she had attended church as a child. What do you think motivated her? Was this a courageous or a cowardly act? What would you have done?

13. Joanna and her husband are raising their children in two faiths—Mormonism and Judaism. She describes how everyone in the family "knows how to pray in at least two languages." What languages exist in your family? Do you have cultural and spiritual traditions that are unique?

14. Joanna describes her dream of a more welcoming Mormonism where everyone has a place at the table. Is anyone excluded from the table in your faith community, culture, neighborhood, or family? What would it take to bring them in? What might your community lose, and what could it gain?

## ENHANCE YOUR BOOK CLUB

While *The Book of Mormon Girl* is an extremely personal story, Joanna Brooks is also a public speaker who regularly gives talks and lectures about her views. Go to YouTube and watch some clips of her speaking in different public forums. What kind of added insight do you have from listening to her speak?

One purpose of this memoir is to address misunderstandings about Mormonism by creating a more humane and three-dimensional picture of Mormon life and culture. You can continue to learn about a diverse range of Mormon people by viewing self-created profiles at the LDS Church's Mormon.org website and the independent Mormon Women Project site (Mormonwomen.com). On YouTube, you can also see the "It Gets Better at Brigham Young University" video made by and for young gay Mormons.

Throughout the book, Joanna talks about insights that she wishes she could share with her younger self. Is there someone in your life for whom you could be a mentor?

Food plays an important cultural role in Joanna's home. Try making some of the Pioneer Day recipes she describes and serve them to the rest of the group. Joanna and her friends sometimes hold Mormon Desserts parties celebrating the kinds of desserts they remember eating as children at church parties: most included lots of Jell-O and Cool Whip!

Here's a classic Joanna's friend Chelsea in Salt Lake City brought to a Mormon Desserts party:

**Strawberry Pretzel Jell-O Dessert**

2 cups crushed pretzels
3 T sugar
½ cup butter, melted
one 8 oz. package of cream cheese, softened
¾ cup sugar
one (8 oz.) carton Cool Whip
one (6 oz.) package strawberry Jell-O
2 cups boiling water
one (20 oz.) package frozen strawberries (use fresh if in season)

Combine and press pretzels, sugar, and butter into a 9" × 13"–pan. Bake at 400 degrees for 8 to 10 minutes. Allow crust to cool. Blend cream cheese, sugar, and Cool Whip. Spread on crust. Mix together Jell-O, water, and strawberries. Spread on top of Cool Whip blend. Refrigerate overnight if possible.

## A CONVERSATION WITH THE AUTHOR

**What are the questions you get asked the most about being a Mormon? What are the biggest misconceptions that you wanted to rectify with this book?**

From its beginnings in the 1830s, Mormonism has always attracted attention, curiosity, and misunderstanding. During the late-nineteenth century especially, Mormons were depicted in American newspapers and political cartoons as a dangerous and murderous polygamous sect. Some of those images persist in the American imagination to this day. One of the ways Mormons have coped with a broad misunderstanding of our faith is to try to project an image of ourselves as being perfectly All-American, with big, monogamous, hard-working, happy families. Think of the Osmonds! Think of Mitt and Ann Romney and their five sons! The truth of who we are lies somewhere between the extremes. Mormons take pride in our distinctive history and comfort in our faith. But we too are regular human beings who struggle with ordinary life challenges. We live in every state in the United States and country around the world. And there is growing diversity within the faith. Not all of us look, think, feel, or believe the same way, even as we all belong to the Mormon tradition.

**You describe a wariness in the Mormon community to share too much with the outside world. How did it feel to share your story with your friends and family? Were you surprised by any of the reactions they had?**

Lots of Mormons are wary about sharing tender or private elements of our faith with non-Mormons. There's a general fear that what we consider tender and meaningful will be ridiculed by strangers; ridicule has long been a part of Mormon experience. There are also controversial elements of Mormon history, like polygamy or the historic ban on priesthood ordination for people of African descent, that Mormons ourselves feel embarrassed by or deeply ambivalent about. It's not easy to talk about these subjects even in our own communities, let alone with people who don't belong to the faith—and yet so much media attention focuses on these hot-buttons! Over the last year or two, as public interest in Mormonism has grown, I've written a great deal about Mormonism for the public and appeared on radio and television. I have always tried to speak candidly and humanely about my faith. My experience has been that if one approaches sensitive topics with dignity, humanity, candor, and even a bit of humor, it bridges misunderstandings and humanizes all participants in the conversation. I'd say good experiences outnumber ridicule by a ten-to-one margin.

As for my family and friends, I always say that no one asks

to have a writer in the family. The LDS community tends to be quite conservative, so I know that my willingness to share my story has brought some pressure upon my family. I also know for a fact that my mother reads every word I publish, and yet though she and I talk frequently, we never really talk about my writing—not even this book! I hope that she and all the good Mormon people I grew up with can see in these pages my fondness for all they taught me and the memories they created. My church youth leaders especially gave of themselves so generously; it wasn't easy teaching young people about doctrine or sexual morality or even camping! But they did, and I am grateful. I should also say that the Mormon congregation I belong to now is very kind and accepting of me and my family, and I am grateful for them as well.

**What kinds of conversations has the book elicited? What would you say to readers who have their own personal stories that they want to share but are concerned about how people might react?**

I've gotten lovely mail from young Mormon women especially, who tell me that my story has helped them feel less alone. That's deeply satisfying to me, especially because I remember how alone I once felt. There were so few books in which I found anything that resembled or spoke to my own experience. When I was very young, there was, of course, *Marie Osmond's Guide to Beauty, Health & Style*, but Marie was way out of my league! In college, I found environmentalist Terry Tempest Williams's book *Refuge: An Unnatural History of Family and Place*, in which she talks about how her family's Mormon faith taught her to question authority. That made an impression on me. One of the greatest lessons I have learned in writing *The Book of Mormon Girl* is that admitting our own differences, vulnerabilities, and struggles can be a powerful act. Of course, you might feel afraid or ashamed. Courage doesn't mean being free from fear; it means learning to work through fear and speak even when we are afraid. I believe that when we do so, we give others the courage to speak more honestly about their own vulnerabilities and struggles as well. No one should be the only one who feels like she has ever made a mistake or struggled with her ideals or taken a path different than the one expected of her. Our stories can shelter and keep each other company as we learn from our experiences.

**In chapter 11 of the book, you describe some profound disagreements you have with certain actions of the LDS Church, but say that you are not giving up. How do you reconcile these conflicting emotions, and what steps are you taking to change the faith from the inside? What advice do you have for others in similar positions?**

Change tends to come very slowly to the LDS Church. There is a strong sense of respect for authority and hierarchy;

more orthodox Mormons might say that real change can only come when top church leaders direct it. But I have also seen many remarkable changes happen among rank-and-file Mormons over the last decades. Mormon scholars and historians have done valuable research into Mormon history that acknowledges the human side of our tradition, including its human flaws. Mormon feminists, gay and lesbian Mormons and their families and allies, and Mormons who may not be literal believers but still cherish the faith have also reached out to one another and offered support and companionship. I am very proud of the brave gay and lesbian Mormons—even students at Brigham Young University—who have found the courage to share their stories. Their courage lights a way to greater compassion and understanding within our faith community.

**Throughout the book, you talk about things that you wish someone had told you when you were growing up. What do you think the most important lesson is, for young Mormons but also for any young reader?**

I always think back to the story of Joseph Smith, the founder of the Mormon faith. When he was just fourteen years old, he harbored deep questions about the religions available to him. None felt right, and he read a scripture in the New Testament that said, "If any of you lack wisdom, let him ask of God." And he did. Joseph Smith went into the woods and prayed for guidance. That is the story of how Mormonism started—it all started when a courageous fourteen-year-old followed the questioning, seeking spirit inside of him. There is a powerful lesson there for all of us. Don't be afraid to ask big questions. Don't be afraid to trust the leadings inside of you. That's the way to truth.

**What are the biggest difficulties in raising your children in an interfaith household? What are the biggest rewards? Do you have any advice for people in a similar position?**

The biggest difficulties so far are very practical ones: we're busy! We're busy doing two sets of holidays! We're busy doing two sets of everything! I know that more serious challenges may lie ahead. Many Jewish people especially have real reservations about raising children in two faith traditions, and I want to acknowledge the seriousness of those reservations. But it was simply impossible for me not to give my children a Mormon faith education, and it was equally impossible for me to deny them a Jewish education, identity, and connection to their Jewish ancestors. David and I tell the girls that being members of an interfaith family means that they have to learn twice as much as the other kids. Religion is about responsibility to a community and a tradition, and we've got to be doubly responsible. David and I have also learned that as interfaith family parents we have to take full responsibility for our children's spiritual education. We can't simply rely on a single institution—be it a church or a synagogue—to teach them. It has to start at our dinner table. We try to infuse our daily lives with a living sense of these two religious worlds—their joys, their demands, their struggles, their foods, their humor, their values. It is up to us.